"I really like the idea of negotiation and asking f(problems in social communication. When I was a mistakes, mother quietly told me what I was doing When I work with clients, I ask lots of questions so that I know exactly what the client expects from the completed design project. This insightful book will help many individuals to have better social relationships."

—*Temple Grandin, author of* Thinking in
Pictures *and* The Way I See It, *USA*

"Brian R. King delivers an engaging and perhaps complete guide to the mind of folks like us. King is a fellow spectrumite and fellow spectrumite parent of spectrum kids; but it is his vocation as a social worker and counselor that wraps King's content into a wonderful addition to the growing library of great books about the entire autism spectrum."

—*Michael John Carley, Executive Director, The Global and
Regional Asperger Syndrome Partnership (GRASP); Executive
Director, Asperger Syndrome Training and Employment Partnership
(ASTEP); and author of* Asperger's from the Inside Out, *USA*

"This is one book I shall be highly recommending and one that I shall be dipping into regularly for its wisdom and truth. Coping with autism is often likened to a roller coaster ride. *Strategies for Building Successful Relationships with People on the Autism Spectrum* provides a model communication highway on which to travel the autism journey, and as the mother of a son with ASD I can certainly relate to that."

—*K.I. Al-Ghani, special educational needs teacher
and author of* Learning About Friendship *and*
From Home to School with Autism, *UK*

"Brian R. King's *Strategies for Building Successful Relationships with People on the Autism Spectrum* is an indispensable contribution to the field of 'inside-out' books written by autism spectrum self-advocates. What could be more valuable to parents, family, and friends than understanding the emotional importance of relationships when viewed through the autism prism?"

—*William Stillman, author of* Autism and the God
Connection *and* Empowered Autism Parenting, *USA*

"In this insightful and easy-to-read book, Brian R. King explains what it feels like to have autism, providing us with the means to a deeper understanding of those on the spectrum. Brian offers tips and strategies in order to best assist a child with autism to become his or her own person, respecting differences and building on strengths. All parents want their children to have meaningful relationships, and in [this book] Brian shares his expert advice in this domain. Brian's perspective is unique and well informed: he is on the spectrum, is married to a person on the spectrum, is the father of three boys on the spectrum, and is an experienced social worker. We have much to learn from him."

—*Chantal Sicile-Kira, author of* Autism Life Skills,
Adolescents on the Autism Spectrum, Autism Spectrum
Disorders, *and* 41 Things to Know About Autism, *USA*

"Brian's book presents a wealth of ideas and strategies for communicating and relating in a new way with the spectrumites in your life. Throw out the star charts and the social scripts. Those never worked, and never will. Bring in the strategies. They do work. I can vouch for them, because I am now using them with my own family, and the results have been positive and immediate... Brian's book will help you understand your loved ones as never before. And I predict you'll understand yourself a lot better too."

—Joan Matthews, mother of James Williams,
a young adult on the spectrum, USA

"Mr. King has created a conversation between people on the spectrum, their families, and advocates with clarity, depth, wisdom, and insight. His advice is both profound and infinitely practical. You'll want to keep this book handy and refer to it again and again."

—*Rudy Simone, author of* Aspergirls *and* 22
Things a Woman Must Know If She Loves a
Man with Asperger's Syndrome, *USA*

STRATEGIES FOR BUILDING
Successful Relationships with People on the Autism Spectrum

of related interest

First Steps in Intervention with Your Child with Autism
Frameworks for Communication
Phil Christie, Elizabeth Newson, Wendy Prevezer and Susie Chandler
Illustrated by Pamela Venus
ISBN 978 1 84905 011 1

Social Communication Cues for Young Children with Autism
Spectrum Disorders and Related Conditions
How to Give Great Greetings, Pay Cool
Compliments and Have Fun with Friends
Tarin Varughese
ISBN 978 1 84905 870 4

Learning About Friendship
Stories to Support Social Skills Training in Children with
Asperger Syndrome and High Functioning Autism
K.I. Al-Ghani
Illustrated by Haitham Al-Ghani
ISBN 978 1 84905 145 3

60 Social Situations and Discussion Starters to Help Teens on
the Autism Spectrum Deal with Friendships, Feelings, Conflict
and More
Seeing the Big Picture
Lisa A. Timms
ISBN 978 1 84905 862 9

Social Skills for Teenagers and Adults with Asperger Syndrome
A Practical Guide to Day-to-Day Life
Nancy J. Patrick
ISBN 978 1 84310 876 4

STRATEGIES FOR BUILDING
Successful Relationships with People on the Autism Spectrum

LET'S RELATE!

BRIAN R. KING

Forewords by Liane Holliday Willey and Susan Giurleo

Jessica Kingsley *Publishers*
London and Philadelphia

First published in 2012
by Jessica Kingsley Publishers
116 Pentonville Road
London N1 9JB, UK
and
400 Market Street, Suite 400
Philadelphia, PA 19106, USA

www.jkp.com

Library of Congress Cataloging in Publication Data
King, Brian R. (Brian Raymond), 1969-
  Strategies for building successful relationships with people on the autism
spectrum : let's relate / Brian R. King ; forewords by Liane Holliday Willey
and Susan Giurleo.
      p. cm.
  Includes bibliographical references.
  ISBN 978-1-84905-856-8
  1. Autism. 2. Autistic people--Family relationships. I. Title.
  RC553.A88K52 2012
  649'.152--dc23
                                              2011011622

British Library Cataloguing in Publication Data
A CIP catalogue record for this book is available from the British Library

ISBN 978 1 84905 856 8

Printed and bound in the United States

To my best friend (you know who you are).

To my sons, Zachary, Aidan, and Connor:

You are my heroes and you inspire me every day to help prepare the world for you as I help prepare you for the world.

Contents

Part 2 Creating Relationships that Work for Both of Us

Foreword

by Liane Holliday Willey

I first met Brian R. King through our Facebook connection. Immediately I was impressed with his words of wisdom to those who sought his counsel and his very kind personality. Mostly I was impressed because he was so accessible and personable. Happily, Brian's book impresses me in much the same way as our Facebook friendship does. It is filled with all kinds of support, strategies and suggestions, and personality. Ultimately, what we have here in *Strategies for Building Successful Relationships with People on the Autism Spectrum: Let's Relate!* is a fascinating tour into the big wide world of autism and beyond with Brian R. King as our host and guide.

The book begins by describing what Brian felt when he first heard he had Asperger's syndrome (AS). With great honesty, he describes the initial frustration upon hearing he has what too many consider a disability...the self-consciousness that comes when he thinks he will be discovered as being too different, too odd...and the worries that stem from his not knowing what the scary future might hold once the reality sets in that life will never be predictable or easy. The book continues, wrapping its way around a host of new ideas on how life with autism spectrum disorder (ASD) can be successfully navigated to include a gentle cohesiveness with neurotypicals.

I imagine many people will relate to Brian's early stories of his life with Asperger's syndrome. And I'd like to personally thank him for including some tough stuff that couldn't have been easy to recall, not to mention writing about it for others to read. As the victim of bullying and a youngster so glued to his routine, Brian had a sadly all too typical Aspie response to the world around him. He was often confused, slow to process and anxious all at the same time. Brian struggled throughout his adolescence and well into early adulthood, not knowing why the world tossed him about so roughly. Like so many of us on the spectrum, he didn't come to his diagnosis of AS until his child was diagnosed with an ASD. It was then he was able to sit down and revisit his past: an activity that brought him closure while simultaneously opening a door to a world of new insight and understanding. With that new insight, he began to decode what it means to be neurotypical not just to satisfy his own living needs, but mostly so that his sons (all of who are on the spectrum) would avoid the pits their father stumbled over or was pushed into.

Even though readers are likely to find similarities between Brian's tale and their own, Brian reminds us we all have our own autism fingerprint, our own tale that makes us our own best expert. I like that. It means we have the power to take control of who we are and how we want to live. Empowerment is a good thing, especially when we add in a dose of accountability for our own actions or as Brian puts it, when we no longer "let life happen to us."

Realizing the importance of working with each person with ASD as an individual, Brian started a mentoring practice for folks on the spectrum. He is qualified to do this not just because he is an Aspie himself and the father of three ASD boys, but also because he holds a Master's in social work. He has the experience and the education to teach us a few new things about education and life skills for people on the spectrum.

It is interesting to read the strategies you will find in this book. Let me correct that, it is interesting to read the strategies for ASD life and happiness you will find in this book. You see, Brian anchors his insight from the inside out, if you will. Looking from the ASD person's point of view, individual neurology and independent reaction to his or her environment, Brian is able to piece together workable solutions to many ASD challenges. Never, however, does he offer a "one size fits all" solution. Rather, what we find are numerous practical thoughts on how to gently lead a person with ASD to discover a life plan that fits just right.

One of my favorite chapters in the book is Chapter 5, titled "My Senses Don't Play Well with Others, Including Me." Sensory integration is not discussed with the frequency of social skills and it is about time this changes. Like Brian, I maintain that if a person does not have a well-regulated and calm sensory system, there is very little chance the person can be moved to understand the social and language exchanges society demands of its people. Kudos to Brian for his analysis of the sensory system. I suggest you read this chapter a few times!

Of course the theme of the book is relationship building and indeed Brian fills it with grand insight into how people on the spectrum can form relationships with one another and how people in the neurotypical world can help us form relationships with them. It's fascinating to hear Brian discuss what makes relationships work and what makes them tick. Honestly, he brings up ideas and thoughts that had never occurred to me and I'm grateful for that.

At first glance, I wasn't sure to whom I would most recommend this book. By the time I finished the book the answer was clear. This book is for anyone who wants to be better informed about ASD, the challenges and the joys. It is for teachers, parents, and people on the spectrum to ponder and soak in. Trust me, *Strategies for Building Successful Relationships with People on the Autism Spectrum* will have an impact on all who read it.

Liane Holliday Willey, EdD
Author of Pretending to be Normal: Living with
Asperger's Syndrome *and* Asperger Safety Skills for
Women: How to Save a Perfectly Good Female Life

Foreword

by Susan Giurleo

In *Strategies for Building Successful Relationships with People on the Autism Spectrum: Let's Relate!*, Brian King gives parents, grandparents, siblings, teachers, and therapists a rare and important gift. He gives us a window into how people on the spectrum experience the social world, and what strategies we can all use to facilitate healthy, reciprocal, mutually beneficial relationships with each other—spectrumite (person on the autism spectrum) and neurotypical (the average person) alike.

Brian has dedicated over twenty years to studying, observing, and implementing communication strategies that help him, his wife, their three children, and his clients all experience positive relationships. Every member of Brian's immediate family is on the autism spectrum, and they work together to understand one another, resolve misunderstandings, and help each other feel important, loved, and respected. Brian's stories of how he and his wife, Cathy, work together to relate to each other and their boys are inspiring.

Brian courageously shares his journey as a child growing up, undiagnosed with autism until adulthood. It is fascinating to discover that the catalyst for his commitment to understand the social world came before he was diagnosed and he describes his learning process and social experimentation to highlight the complexities of social relationships to those with social and sensory challenges.

One of the themes of *Strategies for Building Successful Relationships with People on the Autism Spectrum* is how people's varying sensory systems influence their ability to communicate and engage in social interactions. This insight alone will vastly improve your ability to interact with everyone in your social world, not just those on the spectrum.

By sharing how the sensory system influences communication, Brian allows the reader to better understand why spectrumites behave in apparently quirky ways in social situations. Once we understand that the avoidance of certain social situations and norms has a clear reason and function, it makes it so much easier to move forward to relating.

Brian encourages us to examine our assumptions about connection, communication, and relationships. He sets us on a course to move beyond teaching our children and loved ones to follow rote social scripts and engage in confusing, sometimes painful communication patterns, and he shows us how to interact with our loved ones through mutual respect and commitment to clarify, negotiate, and work together toward healthy connection. His strategies can free us all, spectrumites and neurotypicals alike, from stiff, stilted behavioral interventions that rely on someone becoming "compliant," and gives us the tools to let our loved ones be who they are *and* engaged in healthy communication.

Brian's work is revolutionary. He is the "autism insider" who cracked the communication code for himself, his family, and now for the rest of us who love, know, and work with people on the autism spectrum.

If you ever felt confused, frustrated, or overwhelmed about how to reach out to someone on the autism spectrum, Brian's book gives you the tools to address struggles with tantrums, accepting the word "no," and managing impulsivity.

More importantly, Brian shares straightforward ways to help you encourage a spectrumite's self-reliance, promote positive self-esteem, engage in problem solving, and minimize the impact of the repeated criticism of others. These insights are true gifts.

If you know and love someone on the autism spectrum, so much of what Brian shares will resonate and inform your relationships.

This book gives all of us a clear vision of what it means to live as someone on the autism spectrum and how we, neurotypicals and spectrumites, can work together to get along, communicate, and enjoy each other's contributions and company.

Susan Giurleo
Clinical Psychologist
December 2010

Acknowledgments

To walk the road of life on the autism spectrum is definitely an experience of walking the road less traveled. Through all of its ups and downs, I have had the honor of crossing paths with others who have helped me on my journey.

Michael John Carley, for his continually prodding me to "write the book already" and for always encouraging me to share my thoughts with the spectrum community.

Laura Dessauer, for helping me discover how being myself was the best service I could offer my clients.

Dena Gassner, a fellow spectrumite, who inspires me with her brilliance, passion, and tireless commitment to helping the rest of us get the resources we need.

Susan Giurleo, for helping me see the forest beyond the trees while compelling me to contribute to the spectrum community in new and exciting ways.

Temple Grandin, for writing the Foreword to my book *I'm an Aspie*. Temple epitomizes what it means to be a role model.

Jill Holman, for being an empowered parent who created a small parent group when one didn't exist that has grown into several hundred members. I began attending her group for support when I first learned my son and I were on the spectrum.

Chantal Sicile-Kira, for selflessly helping me find new avenues for sharing my experiences with others and for being a kind and generous friend.

Susan Moreno, for taking a chance on an unknown adult spectrumite and allowing me to participate on a discussion panel at a conference for the autism spectrum. The impact of my contribution that day created a buzz that began the journey to where I am today. That single event began my road to today and the book you have in your hands. Susan is one of those people who has earned my deepest respect and admiration.

Stephen Shore, for being a kind and gentle soul, who has generously shared his time and wisdom with me over the years. More than once he has helped me navigate the increased pressures and opportunities this journey has provided.

William Stillman, for being a champion of seeing the beauty and wisdom of the autism experience and for seeing in me a beauty that needed to be shared.

James Williams and his mother, Joan Matthews, for being so accessible in the early months of my spectrum awareness, guiding me on the path of self-acceptance and empowerment. And for seeing me through to this point as Joan graciously edited this book for publication.

Liane Holliday Willey, for continuing to be a tireless advocate for what spectrumites have to offer this world and for doing me the honor of writing a Foreword for this book.

A very special thanks to:

David Steele, Frankie Dioran, and Bill Paglia-Sheff, for helping me discover potential I never knew I had. Then helping me turn that potential into something bigger than myself.

Introduction

Imagine living in a world where nonverbal communication doesn't exist. That's the world in which those on the autism spectrum live. For thirty-five years of my life I struggled to understand why others seemed to form close relationships with ease while I continued to clean up one social mess after another.

When the term "autism spectrum" entered my life, I finally found an explanation for what had been preventing so many friendships from lasting. The more I studied the more I was able to discover the missing pieces in the puzzle of my social life. I read countless books and articles insisting that social conventions such as eye contact, chitchat, and working in groups were considered nonnegotiable means of social success.

What was more puzzling was my discovery that those insisting that I make eye contact, engage in chitchat, etc., couldn't explain why these things were necessary or if they truly were necessary. They were simply common, universally accepted as necessary, and weren't examined in terms of their actual effectiveness in improving communication and connection.

No one could offer me a reason to put myself through such torment, other than, because that's how it's done. I simply didn't get it; I couldn't determine the logic behind why others communicate as they do. So I set out to find a way to work around the social conventions that would allow me to communicate effectively without my difficulty decoding nonverbal communication getting in the way. I wanted to figure out how to communicate in a way that made nonverbal communication unnecessary.

As a father, I have the additional responsibility and commitment of preparing my three sons on the autism spectrum for the world. I need to help them realize, first, that people on the spectrum filter life differently from others. Second, they need to learn how to get the information that doesn't make it through that filter, such as nonverbal communication. The way we process information is so profoundly different that if we do not understand the specific gaps in the way our brain takes in information and do not use specific strategies to fill in those gaps, we are going to be socially ineffective our entire lives. Our experiences of being criticized, bullied, ostracized, and called names simply because we do not have the most effective communication tools to get the job done would only become worse. I absolutely had to find a way.

I found a way, several in fact. What I ultimately discovered has amazed me in terms of both the effectiveness of the strategies I will teach you, and also in terms of how they improve the communication and relationships of everyone who uses them, whether they're on the spectrum or not.

One of my greatest discoveries is that reliance on nonverbal communication is actually a significant barrier to communication and not the asset it is touted to be. I'll explain throughout this book why that is the case and what you can do instead.

What I have discovered goes well beyond what I will be sharing in this book, but the foundation I'll be providing will help you understand what it means to communicate and connect to another person in a way you never imagined. You will probably discover that the way you were told relationships work and must work is filled with rules that actually make things worse and increase the number of arguments and misunderstandings you experience.

An important theme of this book is that *all relationships are negotiated*. The quality of the relationships you are currently in, whether with a spouse, a friend, or your child, is exactly what you have agreed to, whether you realize it or not. We'll discuss how negotiations are made with particular focus on negotiating the relationship you want to have with your child on the autism spectrum.

The key is to learn how to negotiate a partnership that meets the needs of both people, instead of the power struggle so many parents of children on the autism spectrum have become resigned to. I aim to teach you how to agree on the way your relationship will work, by negotiating how to give each other feedback on what is and isn't working in a way you'll be eager and grateful to hear. With this approach there's no need to be afraid the other person will get angry with you for being honest.

There's a reason why behavior plans and star charts are often ineffective and you will learn how you can make them a thing of the past. When your children tell you the social skills group you're sending them to is a waste of time, they may be right. It is possible to have a close, connected relationship without making eye contact, reading nonverbal cues or knowing what the other person is thinking. They'll be able to be themselves in a way that makes it easier to be in a relationship with them.

The end goal for our work as parents is to prepare our children for the world. When you are the parent of a child on the autism spectrum you have the added responsibility of preparing the world for him. Our children won't be successful by becoming normal, fitting in or being indistinguishable from their peers. They'll be successful by learning how to negotiate partnerships with other people that allow them to be themselves and make their greatest contribution to society, one person at a time.

I want to take a moment to congratulate you for reading this book. The strategies I'll be teaching you require commitment to apply until you've mastered them. You're raising a child on the spectrum so you already have commitment. I'm sure you know a lot of people who talk about wanting a better relationship with their child, but who never do anything about it. Or maybe they start strong but their motivation fades. You've been given an opportunity to learn how to improve your communication, to improve the relationships in your life, and you took action, you showed up, and I really want to honor you for that. Too many people continue to suffer in life because they make excuses instead of taking responsibility. Clearly you are not one of those people and I congratulate you on doing that for yourself and those in your life who will benefit from your commitment.

Compiling this book was daunting for me. In addition to being on the spectrum I also experience significant challenges due to attention deficit disorder (ADD) and you will see it throughout this book. You'll see repetitions and jumps from one idea to the next, without transitions that are as smooth as you're used to. The important thing to remember is to focus on how to apply the ideas described herein. That is where the value ultimately lies.

I will explain many of the strategies through dialogues between various parents and their children. Though based on actual people I've worked with over the years, these dialogues, the descriptions of the people and their circumstances, are composites in order to protect their anonymity.

I also want the parents and educators reading this to be prepared for the strong and often blunt tone I use when describing interactions between parents and children and teachers and students. The fact is they are based on common experiences in households and classrooms. I have no intention of indicting the teaching profession and there are no grounds for a teacher reading this to feel I'm talking about you if what I describe doesn't apply to you.

For those educators who do their job well, you deserve to hold your head up high when you read the examples of how others have chosen to back down while you decided to step up. My life and the lives of my sons owe much of their success to the fantastic teachers we have encountered throughout our lives. It is because of the experience of profound change that can occur when people take the time to get it right, that I must be unapologetic for mentioning when others insist upon doing it wrong. There is far too much at stake to beat around the bush.

I want to close this introduction by sharing the important role that teachers have played in my life. I'd like you to think about the most valuable lesson your favorite teacher(s) taught you. For me, it was that I matter. I've been accused by many of giving teachers a bad rap. Mostly by those who don't pay close attention to what I say and write. I make reference to teaching styles, approaches to teaching and the like. I spend a lot of time writing about correcting poor parenting styles but it doesn't make me anti-parent, does it?

The unfortunate reality is that I am called upon by parents to help advocate in situations where school staff and administrators seem fully committed only to being proved right. They seem to me to be unteachable and, in the worst cases, more interested in not helping. Sounds crazy, right? But it happens.

But then there are the stars of the profession, the teacher that stands out in your life for one important reason, because she made you feel like you stood out in hers. It seems to me that success nowadays is often measured by tests that do not take creativity into account. This makes it increasingly difficult to help a child learn and celebrate the things that make him shine. But it is still possible.

I consulted with a team of teachers recently who were being entrusted with welcoming a young boy (on the spectrum) into their school and into their classroom. They were preparing to improve significantly upon his previous school experience, which was traumatic. I'm always anxious prior to such meetings because I never know what I'll encounter in terms of the receptivity of those I'll be working with.

I've met those who want to tell me how wrong I am and then those who genuinely want to learn from me as much as I want to learn from them. Let's face it; I'm not a schoolteacher. So I rely entirely on them to describe their experience while I describe the experience of students on the spectrum. That's the only way to find the middle ground.

Well, the team I met with recently was a breath of fresh air. It's been a long time since I've met a group of educators this committed to getting it right on behalf of one student. What I really enjoyed hearing were their ideas on how to include the rest of the class in very specific ways to work together for this young man's success.

Thinking back, I was raised in an era before the autism spectrum was even a term. I slipped through the cracks more often than not, seldom got the support I needed, was bullied mercilessly at times, and could have easily curled up in a corner and given up.

But while it felt like no one cared whether I lived or died much of the time, there was a select group of people throughout my life who took notice. Who took the time and made the effort to see to it that I knew I mattered. Who were these people? Teachers.

In third grade my art teacher Mrs. Z. saw that I was very self-critical and often quit before I even started. She was the first to identify me as "my own worst enemy." She was right, and she never gave up on me. I remember her calm demeanor and her patience as she helped me find my way through the various art projects. I don't remember any of the art projects and am not particularly interested in art. What I remember was the relationship. Now I see my middle son light up when it's art class day at school. He has an artistic talent I never had and I am thrilled that he has the experience of being nurtured in that way.

In sixth grade there was Miss G. I had her for music class but at some point she noticed I was dabbling in poetry. She read every poem I wrote as though it were the most magnificent thing ever written. It wasn't that she was giving me inflating praise, what she was doing was encouraging me to continue and refine what I was writing. Look how far I've come.

In seventh and eight grade there was Mrs. C. She was my counselor and very much a teacher. She never asked me to go any faster than I needed to to make things work. Whenever I'd take one step forward and two steps back, she was there to understand, validate my frustrations and help me move forward again.

Then there's the greatest teacher I ever had. I was lost through my first two years of high school until in my junior year when I met Mrs. A. I didn't have her as a classroom teacher; instead she was the faculty advisor for a group I was in that focused on bringing drug abuse awareness programs to the grade schools.

This group was my first exposure to public service and Mrs. A. saw abilities in me that she was compelled to nurture. She was my greatest mentor and now, more than twenty years after high school graduation, she has become a trusted friend. She retired this past school year and we had a conversation by phone in which I told her of all the ways she contributed to the person I've become. Most of all, I made it very clear to her that when she looks back at her legacy as a teacher, she can think of me.

The greatest lesson I learned from each of these amazing teachers was that I had more to offer them than just my undivided attention. There are teachers that seem rushed and more focused on completing tasks than relating to their students. Then there are those who realize the power of their relationships with their students. I've benefited from it, my two elder sons are now benefiting from it. And I always smile when I hear stories from clients of their experiences with those who truly get it.

Teachers are some of the most phenomenal multitaskers in the world. They work long hours, for less money than they're worth, and often receive far more criticism than they ever deserve (I'm sorry for my part in that). They continue each and every day to show up and work their butts off in the hope that they can help the student who just needs that opportunity to shine.

Who was your favorite teacher? What was the most valuable lesson that he or she taught you? As I now do my part to pay it forward, I hope to teach you how to have a life-changing relationship as a parent with your child, and as a teacher with your student. Enjoy.

Part I What It Feels Like to Be on the Autism Spectrum

Chapter I

We Have Autism

There are many books about how difficult it was to grow up on the autism spectrum and not learning about it until you were an adult. How you wondered what your life would have been like had you known sooner. Therefore I'm not going to waste your time giving you more of the same. I'm far more interested in improving upon the past instead of dwelling on it. Instead, I'm going to focus on how I found out and what I did next. After all, what I did next is the reason you're reading this book. So I want to get there as quickly as possible.

It started with my son

I was thrilled the day I learned I was going to be a father. Especially because I had been told I might never be able to have children. I was diagnosed with testicular cancer shortly before my high school graduation. I was informed by my doctor that the intensive chemotherapy I received to cure it might have rendered me infertile. So I lived all those years knowing I might never have children. Then came Zachary.

He was smart, precocious and full of life. We were so proud to see him enter first grade in what was sure to be a bright academic career. It didn't take long for everything to fall apart. Zach was our only child for four years so we had no other point of reference. As far as we knew, he was just like any other kid. We didn't discover any of his challenges until he started first grade, because up until that point, having me as his father, he was never really put into very intense social situations.

I didn't interact with neighbors or hang out with people much. I stuck to family so Zach had a lot of familiarity. With the exception of the day care he went to while his mother and I worked, I don't remember Zach having much contact with other kids his age. So when he entered first grade, as far as I knew, everything was fine. I didn't hear much from the school and believed no news was good news. Then about two or three months into the school year, I received a phone call from his teacher in the middle of my workday, and she described an incident on a field trip.

The class was touring a museum, and everything was going according to plan. They had an unscheduled change in the itinerary when offered an opportunity to listen to an eighty-year-old gentleman speak about his experience in a one-room schoolhouse. Zach began to get very agitated, as this man droned on and on about his memories. So halfway through the presentation, Zach stood up, turned around, looked at his teacher, and started screaming, "This is boring, this is terrible, I want to leave right now. This is an unscheduled change, you didn't tell me about this." His teacher said she had a hard time containing her laughter because she agreed with him. It was at that point she realized she needed to call and tell me things she'd noticed about Zach and some difficulties she'd been having in the classroom.

She shared that pretty much since the beginning of the school year, Zach "tends to be the timekeeper in the classroom. He wants to know when everything is going to start, and when it's going to stop, and if it doesn't stop when I say it's going to stop, he reminds me that it's time to stop and move on to the next thing.

He always wants to know what's going to happen first, and what order it's going to happen in. He's very meticulous in his day."

That reminded me of something I noticed with Zach whenever we were in the car. I'd have him sit behind me but he'd always lean over and watch the clock on the dashboard the whole time. He'd always ask me how long it was going to take to get where we were going, and the closer it got to the time I told him, he'd remind me and ask if we were there yet. If my calculations were off, he made a point of telling me how wrong I was.

After describing Zach's timekeeping efficiency, it was the teacher's next statement that really caught my attention. She said, "If there's an unexpected change in his day, he panics." While getting my Master's degree in social work, I learned a lot about human differences—I don't like the term *disorder*—and one of them was autism. So when she was describing the different things Zach had been doing, I remembered what I'd learned about autism. From what I'd remembered learning and the difficulties associated with it, it was difficult to consider this in relationship to Zach. Hoping that I was wrong in my assumption, I jokingly said, "Well, maybe he's high-functioning autistic." And she said, "Well, I think maybe he is." I was speechless for a few seconds and then asked, "What do we do now?" She said she needed to fill out some paperwork, after which there would be a team meeting to discuss evaluating Zach to see if additional supports would be helpful for him in the classroom.

It's called Asperger's

That started everything moving, but unfortunately, the teacher's phone call to me was a little too late as Zach was quickly reaching his saturation point in the school year. Though we'd had our meeting during which they agreed to do a case study to see if Zach met the school's criteria for autism, a case study which the law said they had sixty days to complete, it was clear Zach's ability to manage the school environment wasn't going to last sixty days.

So I became proactive and got a referral for a child psychologist from Zach's pediatrician, and then an occupational therapist (OT).

In the first session with the psychologist, Zach was doing things I hadn't seen before. He was walking around the room touching everything and wouldn't stop when asked. He began playing with toys he could spin and became very excited when he made them spin. Even to the point of bouncing on the tips of his toes. He reached in front of the psychologist to tap keys on her computer as though she wasn't there. That and many other things allowed her to quickly determine that Zach fell on the Asperger's part of the autism spectrum.

I have Asperger's?

It was the first visit to the occupational therapist that threw up the red flags for me. She gave me a lengthy questionnaire to complete, and while reading it, I quickly began to wonder whether these questions were about Zach or myself. I could relate to the questions about holding railings while going up staircases, shying away from bright lights, feeling queasy in situations where there's a lot of motion like riding in a car, or if you're walking along and something moves, do you move with it—and I looked at her, and said, "Can I have another one of these to fill out for myself, because I think this is me, too." And she said, "Well, didn't you already know?"

I became a little panicky and asked, "What do you mean? Do you think I have this, too?" She quickly realized I didn't know this about myself and nervously backpedaled, saying that she wasn't qualified to diagnose anyone, and encouraged me to follow up with someone for an assessment.

Looking back on that visit, I remember the cramped waiting room with blazingly bright fluorescent lights, odd for the waiting room of an OT clinic. So by the time we were called for our assessment, I was agitated and avoiding eye contact even more because my eyes were so tired from the lights. She must have spotted this.

When we arrived home I ordered a bunch of books on Asperger's and did a lot of research on the internet. Subconsciously I was looking for information that excluded Asperger's as a possibility for myself. At one point I was reading through some criteria for Asperger's on a website and thought for sure I'd found the evidence that excluded me. I asked my wife to come read it and tell me what she thought. She read it and said, "Yep, that's you." I was defensive at first and asked her what she was talking about. She proceeded to describe qualities in me I was oblivious to.

She described my monologuing, having to be right all the time (a characteristic I've done a considerable amount of work to change), my anxiety when unexpected things happen, how I didn't talk to anybody when we got together with her family. I was just going about life, doing my thing, and I'd never given any of this a second thought.

I became fixated on it and had a very hard time making sense of it all. I began thinking about my life and how horrible my childhood was. Why I didn't have friends in grade school. Why I was bullied mercilessly. Why, when I made a wholehearted effort to be liked, to join in, to be one of the crowd, it consistently resulted in disaster. I never could figure out what I was doing wrong. So I spent a lot of time just watching everybody else play. I'd sit on the edge of the playground. I found the ants marching along in a straight line, and they were far more entertaining than sports. So that's how I spent my childhood. I occasionally had a friend here, a friend there. And in school my friend typically was the other outcast that nobody else would play with. So we just kind of hung out together.

And all that time, for so many years, I thought there was something wrong with me. And now with the revelation of Asperger's, I realized the problem did not lie with me. The problem lay with the lack of a fit between me and the rest of the world. The problem was that disconnect. The problem wasn't me and the problem wasn't anybody else. It was that we didn't know how to bridge that gap between us.

When I was finally ready to face this reality I made an appointment with the psychologist who assessed Zach. I remember how anxious I was in the waiting room. The sound seemed louder and my clothes seemed particularly scratchy. When I entered her office, I remember asking her to dim the lights. This moment I'll never forget. I suspect I was struggling to look at her to begin the conversation and she said, "You don't have to look me in the eye if you don't want to. You don't even have to look at me if it'll help."

That pretty much confirmed everything for me. I thanked her for being so considerate and then I told her about my research, my confusion, my childhood, and my anger. She listened very compassionately and reassured me that I was the same person I'd always been and that the only thing that had changed was that I had a lot more answers than I had before.

That was a wonderful thing for her to say but I had a hard time believing it. Being told I had Asperger's made me increasingly self-conscious to the point of paranoia. I was so aware of my eye contact, my fidgeting, and everything else that I became terrified others would spot them and think something was wrong with me. I became depressed and had several sessions with the psychologist to work through it.

Determined to feel other than disordered

The shift in my thinking came as I continued to research on the internet, looking for anything positive to help me feel better about this. Then I came across the website of Stephen Shore and purchased his book *Beyond the Wall*. I also found the website for Liane Holliday Willey and bought her book *Pretending to Be Normal*. I devoured those books when I received them and they were so validating for me that I began to feel less isolated, more at peace with this newly discovered part of myself. I'm even more honored to say that five years later Stephen Shore has become a mentor of mine and generously offers me guidance on how to make my contribution to the spectrum community. As you may have noticed, Liane wrote the Foreword to this book.

It was through Liane's work that I first learned the term *Aspie* which is a word adults with Asperger's use to refer to themselves because the term *Asperger's syndrome* was so negative and invalidated a person's strengths. Then it occurred to me that the label itself was a huge part of the stress I was having.

Though learning I had Asperger's answered a lot of questions for me, it created a huge problem in that it was coupled with the word *syndrome*. My initial research of Asperger's and autism kept leading me to repeated references to *disability, syndrome, disorder, deficits, weaknesses*; how on earth could I possibly begin to feel better about myself if doing so meant I had to embrace such thinking about myself? I was a social worker. If I didn't feel good about myself, how could I help clients feel good about themselves? How can I raise my child, who has just been told he has Asperger's, and say, "Well, dear son, I'm going to raise you to adulthood in spite of your disability, or in spite of this syndrome you're suffering from." What kind of a way is that to raise a child? I just could not embrace that kind of language or thinking about him or myself.

So I worked and worked and worked through my own mind to try and figure out how I could find a middle ground. How could I find the happy medium? How could I not look at myself as a broken normal person and see myself as somebody who is whole, who just happens to have this unique way of interacting with the larger world? So I basically chopped off the *syndrome* part—just using *Asperger's*, or *Aspie*—and made a point of emphasizing his and my strengths.

That mind-set has made it so much easier to embrace being an Aspie as part of who I am. It's not the entirety of who I am. I have many qualities, and Asperger's just happens to be a significant part of my humanity. I think of it as the address where I live on the human spectrum.

In fact, one of the first analogies I heard was from Zach's first-grade teacher. She said we're all snowflakes, similar but each one of us is one of a kind. She told me that to reassure me that she'd always see Zach as an individual, and she did.

These days I don't even think about the label when working with my clients. I just identify their strengths and challenges, find out what they want to accomplish, and help them work through what's standing in the way. You don't need to discuss disorders or syndromes to do that, and my clients make better progress as a result.

In fact, the main reason Asperger's is seen as a syndrome is because of the tendency of the psychiatric community to pathologize difference. Don't get me wrong, I take medication for ADD, and it has changed my life for the better in so many ways. I'm calmer, more focused, more productive. I just don't think it's necessary to refer to a person's personality traits as disordered. It's very shaming for those who receive these labels and then think, "Well, that's it then. I'm broken, I'm disabled. Can't do it, the doctor said so."

I spend so much time helping clients work through the damage of the diagnosis or the label that it often takes a while before we can begin working on building their skill-set. I'd much rather we dropped the *disorder* or *syndrome* from these descriptions and called them *patterns* or *phenomena* or something. Something that isn't so limiting so that those who receive these labels see opportunities instead of dead ends.

How I made peace with my school years

I admit I spent time "what ifing" my past. What if my teachers and parents had known? Would things have been different, would they have been better? I don't know and can't know for sure. I saw no point in fantasizing about a better past when the more compelling question was, "how do I move forward?"

The time I did spend on my past was to make peace with the broken child I grew up thinking I had been. To tell him what a wonderful, special boy he was. How strong he'd been all those years, and to let him know that he doesn't need to be afraid any more. I'll take care of him from now on.

I reflected upon who I was then and I really don't remember playing with anyone in preschool or even being interested. I remember doing my own thing. I only have spotty memories of playing with a smock on, splashing in a water table and not talking to anyone. In kindergarten the one thing I remember most is that it was loud. Kids were always running around and I never knew what I was supposed to be doing.

My mother shared with me that my kindergarten teacher once asked if I was retarded because I moved so slowly and never answered her questions. Well, between not being able to hear her and being overloaded all the time, I'm amazed I accomplished anything.

I walked to and from school each day and, for whatever reason, three boys saw to it that I was miserable each day. They'd stop me and take turns repeatedly pushing me to the ground until they were satisfied. Then they'd let me walk home. Now, looking back, I didn't vary my path home because I liked my routine, same way there, same way back. I liked my structure. I just continued to hope that one day they wouldn't bother me anymore. I think there was one day I did take a different path and I was anxious the whole time because it was a change. A few years ago I learned that one of those boys has spent most of his time since high school in and out of prison. I suspect his childhood was more difficult than he made mine.

I made peace with that time when the end of my first marriage led my sons and me back to my hometown. I enrolled my middle son Aidan in first grade at the very same school. Now a seasoned advocate, I walked those same hallways with greater confidence than I had as a five-year-old. Seeing to it that Aidan received everything he needed to feel safe and confident in that environment did more than I can say to comfort the pains of the past. At times I could feel the five-year-old in me smiling and saying, "Look what I just did."

Grade school bullies

I remember a few times when some of the kids would try and include me in games on the playground during recess, but I'd get overwhelmed pretty quickly. I mean, the faster the game moved, the quicker I would get confused and not know what to do. So I would just stop playing and go sit down. It was just a lot easier to opt out.

I also remember hearing others say I was shy, which was hard to reconcile with always being told to stop talking so much when I was at home. I guess I saved my monologues for my mother and the other adults in my life.

I remember that when I did speak up, I was often told that I was rude and too blunt. People would have such strong reactions to my opinions that after a while it became safer to simply shut up. It's amazing when you find yourself in a context where being yourself is dangerous; you tend to just stand back. The social environment is completely unforgiving. It doesn't allow you to be imperfect.

I was in a small Catholic grade school in a small classroom, so it's not like you can mess up in front of one group and then move on to another one and have a do over. They were keeping score and didn't let me forget any of my less than perfect moments. I had six years of torment there. There were bullies. There were the kids that were very well-to-do and seemed to have a sense of entitlement. They made a point of deciding who was good enough and who wasn't, who was special and who was inferior. I heard every single day exactly where I stood with them.

It got to a point where I was so anxious about the idea of going to school each day that I developed frequent stomachaches. They weren't always bad enough to stay home but sometimes Mom would let me. On several occasions my mom would take me to the doctor to see why I was sick so much. The doctor would say I was fine and I'd be back to the torture of school the next day. The funny thing is that on one occasion I remember being so nervous that when the doctor said I was fine I actually threw up. It ended up buying me a few extra days at home. I don't recommend that strategy for anyone, by the way, I just think it's a funny side note.

The bottom line is, I was called a faker a lot, a wimp and a sickly child, when in reality I was a complete nervous wreck because if I was to leave my home and go to school, I knew it was just a place to survive. Who was going to push me down on the playground today? Who was going to call me names? Who was going to bump my elbow when I was trying to write? It was always a moment-to-moment anticipation of where the next assault was going to come from.

There was one incident in fourth grade when we were standing in line for something and a classmate punched me in the stomach for the heck of it. I remember being doubled over in pain and having difficulty breathing. I'll never forget this, my clueless first-year teacher escorting me to the office saying, "It was probably just a misunderstanding." *No*, I understood perfectly what had just happened to me. There was more than one occasion when my mom wanted to put that teacher through a wall.

I remember another time in sixth grade when the teacher was in the back of the classroom and I was in the front by the teacher's desk getting something. The next thing I knew, a classmate picked up the large wastebasket from the floor next to the teacher's desk, put it over my head, and started banging on it like a drum. The can was large enough that it covered my shoulders as well and was difficult to get off. The banging noise felt like someone punching my eardrums. I did everything I could not to burst into tears. I was so humiliated. The only repercussion for this classmate was that he was told to return to his seat.

The single greatest event that allowed me to make peace with those horrible years was when, after divorcing my first wife, I reconnected with a childhood friend. Cathy and I have known each other since we were four years old and she was quiet like I was. I remember having a crush on her and she was a constant source of reassurance throughout those years.

We lost touch when I transferred to the middle school but I continued to think about her and what a great friend she'd been. I stumbled upon her in a social networking website and the rest, as they say, is history. Cathy and I are happily married and raising the boys together. There will be much more on this throughout the book so hold tight.

Middle school

After sixth grade my parents finally decided that the Catholic school environment wasn't good for me but, not knowing any better, decided that shoving me into a very large public middle school was the solution. Let's just say that the analogy of out of the frying pan, into the fire was an understatement. My recollection of middle school is a complete fog with a few random memories. My mom told me stories about things I would do, and phone calls she would receive from the staff, things that I don't even recall doing. I was so intimidated by the cafeteria—it was noisy, crowded, and a modern study in chaos. Mom said she received phone calls that school staff kept finding me in the bathroom eating my lunch.

I remember that I ended up working with a counselor who did what could be best described as exposure therapy. She'd take me to the threshold of the cafeteria so I could look in and take it in a little bit at a time. I do recall that eventually I was able to go into the cafeteria, sit there, and talk to a few of the kids at the table, but I think it probably took a good six months to get me in there.

I'd like to tangent here to discuss my stance on cafeterias. The way I look at it now is that there is absolutely nothing to be gained from having a child on the spectrum eat in the cafeteria if the child's primary experience of it is survival. Doing so may be in service of the school's needs, but may not be in service of the student's needs. School staff have argued that this is the child's primary opportunity for socializing but this can be problematic as, in my experience, children on the spectrum do not and will not socialize effectively in sensory chaos. Every adult spectrumite that I know prefers quiet gatherings with a few people, maybe under a very structured setting. They don't seek out sensory mosh-pits to get to know each other.

So when you have the school saying, "Well, your child needs to eat in the cafeteria," you may need to answer that no, he doesn't. I had this discussion with a school staff member when touring the school Aidan would be attending for second grade. The staff member happened to be the occupational therapist that would be working with him. She said, "We noticed his previous IEP [Individualized Education Plan] said that he had the option of eating in the office, but we really want him to eat in the cafeteria because that's the primary social opportunity."

I was shocked to hear such an ignorant statement from an OT, who was supposed to have training in the sensory issues of children on the autism spectrum. I was feeling unfiltered that day and wasn't about to have this happen to him so I said very frankly, "Well, that's your opinion. If you don't provide him with other opportunities that are much more in tune with his nervous system and individual needs, that is the fault of the school, and it's not his obligation to accommodate the school's shortcomings. Why on earth should he have to force himself to socialize in a situation that does not work for him because it suits you?"

I hope you will not need to be so blunt, but the point I want to make is that it is crucial to find out what is best for your child.

She was speechless at first. I turned to my son and asked, "Where did you eat lunch last year?" I noticed him stand up a little straighter as he confidently replied, "I ate in the principal's office." I asked, "Is that OK with you or would you like to eat in the cafeteria?" He said, "I want to eat in the office." I then asked him if he ate alone in the office. He said, "Well, I got to bring some friends. And we got to eat lunch together."

I then looked to the OT and said, "We must allow him that because there are going to be days when maybe he's had a rough morning at home, or he didn't sleep well the night before, and he just doesn't have the energy to withstand the cafeteria. He needs to have a Plan B." Now my son is in third grade and prefers the office over the cafeteria. He has on occasion asked to eat in the cafeteria but in the end it is simply too loud for him.

Though I found the cafeteria overloading, I simply resigned myself to it because no one gave me an alternative. I had to be very much a follower in order to survive each day. I did make one or two friends in middle school. However, there was a group of bullies in the cafeteria that took great joy in threatening to beat me up because I would react nervously and then they'd laugh. There were also those who would deliberately bump into me as hard as they could, kick me, or shove me into the lockers during passing periods, and once I remember someone leaning over a railing and spitting on my head.

I finally fought back

The exasperation of the near daily bullying grew and finally reached a breaking point.

There was one boy who notoriously made a point of hitting me with his shoulder as hard as he could every passing period. Then he'd give me a sarcastic grin when I looked at him after he did it. Well, one day I was having a lousy day and couldn't take much more. So when he bumped me that day, I remember grabbing him by the shirt and slamming him up against a locker and yelling, "Don't you ever f***king touch me again."

I vividly remember the look of shock on his face. He walked away and never touched me again. There was another time that I didn't even see it coming. The background of this incident was that I'd been clumsy my entire life and am still to this day. Gym class was the class I knew I'd always be picked last and would contribute next to nothing.

But then, we reached the volleyball section. I was tall, skinny, and had long arms, which became an asset when it came to serving and blocking the ball. I was surprisingly good at it and others took notice. For the first time in my life people wanted me on their team. I was really enjoying this time and it meant a lot to have such social approval. Little did I know that one of the kids in class, who was very athletic and used to a lot of attention, was building up a lot of resentment toward me because he felt I was stealing his thunder.

So in true alpha male fashion he invited his friends to walk home from school with him one day to watch him beat me up. What he didn't know is that my father, who taught hand-to-hand combat in the Army, began instructing me when he learned about the bullying at the middle school. I tend to be very passive and had a hard time contemplating ever using it. The way this scene unfolded was that I saw a group of about ten or more kids walking together behind me; this was very unusual. I, being a creature of habit, walked home the same way every day and saw the same kids. This was clearly different.

I saw the kid in question pointing at me as the group got closer and then suddenly he was in front of me and pushed me, saying, "You think you're pretty cool, huh?" I told him I had no idea what he was talking about. He shoved me again and said, "Come on. Do something if you're so tough." I told him I didn't know why he was mad at me and that I didn't want to fight.

He said, "Too bad," then wrapped his arms around me as he tried to punch me in the kidneys. I broke free, pushed him back, punched him twice in the face, then side-kicked him so hard he flew backwards and fell to the ground.

He stood up, brushed himself off, and said, "Well, I've got to hand it to you, you know how to fight." Then I said, "Can we stop this now?" as I extended my hand for a handshake. He shook my hand and said, "Sure."

Of course, his idiot friends were whining, "Oh, come on," because they wanted to see a fight. So I walked on, occasionally looking over my shoulder to make sure I had enough distance between them and me. Things changed after that.

Though it would have been nice to be able to solve those problems without getting physical, I wasn't picked on quite as much for the rest of middle school. But the coolest thing was what happened the day after the fight. I was approached by a fellow student, someone I didn't know. He told me his name and explained that he had been the best friend of the boy that picked the fight with me. After watching how I conducted myself, he realized what a jerk his friend was and asked if I wanted to hang out sometime. He became my best friend and we were inseparable through high school and we're friends to this day. His friendship has been one of the greatest blessings of my life.

What allowed me to make peace with those years is that my eldest son Zach now attends the same school. He spent many years in various schools for special needs children because the public school system was not giving him what he needed. He was asked if he wanted to try the middle school and took some time to think about it. He eventually said he wanted to try it. In helping prepare him for this transition I had a similar experience to when I supported Aidan in first grade. A series of meetings with those directly responsible for Zach (meetings which included Zach) led to an iron-clad agreement of how he would be supported while at school.

It has been by no means a smooth transition but the days keep getting better and Zach is growing into an amazing young man. An interesting side note is that the school social worker who has been a godsend for Zach in his transition was mentored by the same counselor who helped me all those years ago. Isn't that something?

High school

In high school, fortunately, I found that I was better able to disappear in the crowd. Several different schools fed into the high school so there were a lot of new kids and some of the old cliques and alliances carried over, but there were so many other kids now to contend with, it was almost like they couldn't bother with me anymore, which was a good thing. And I for the most part just kept my mouth shut and followed along and tried not to stand out too much.

I still had the same social awkwardness and did not know how to make friends. My best friend from middle school was very social and almost everyone I met, I met through him. But it was around junior year that I really hit my stride and school started feeling like a place that maybe had more to offer than just a place to survive each day. It was around that time that I discovered my sense of humor, and that I had a talent for accents. I was fascinated by foreign accents, the way they sounded, and the way they felt to speak.

One thing my mom shared with me is that growing up I was a big TV junkie. She said she used to call me "The Jingle Kid" because I would walk around singing the jingles to different commercials. I was fond of quoting movie lines, which my boys have adopted, and especially British humor, such as Monty Python. So in high school, one of my friends (who I suspect is probably somewhere on the spectrum) and I would sit at the same table in the cafeteria at lunch and recite Monty Python skits back and forth. The kids sitting around us at the other tables were in hysterics.

It turns out that when you make people laugh, they don't want to bully you anymore. So I think in many respects finding my sense of humor was a reprieve. So my last two years of high school were a lot easier to deal with.

My high school legacy

There are a few things I want to share that I'm particularly proud of from my high school years. Due to my cafeteria antics, a few of my friends and I were talking one day about how cool it would be if we could all get up on stage and perform for the school. The more we talked about it, the more we wanted to do it. So we approached the choir director, who knew us well, and he said, "Oh, like a variety show." He liked the idea and got permission to proceed. So he, my friends, and I oversaw the auditions, and before long, the first ever variety show was held at my high school. I performed about fifteen minutes of standup comedy, my own material, and everyone in the auditorium cheered loudly when I was done. That was an amazing moment for me. That was in 1987 and I know the school continued to have it for many years after that. I don't know if they're still doing it.

The day after, I was approached by a classmate, who told me of a group of students who went to area grade schools and performed skits about drug abuse prevention and asked if I'd be interested in joining. She and the group's advisor saw me perform at the variety show and were excited about having me join the group.

To cut a long story short, I joined, we dressed up in clown makeup and presented outrageous skits that we wrote ourselves, and it was some of the most fun I've ever had helping others. The group's advisor was a special education teacher who became one of my greatest mentors. She just retired from teaching this year. We talk every now and then and I always remind her how much her guidance and support have meant to me over the years. I often look upon my life with a smile when I think about how blessed I was to have had a few of those diamonds throughout my life that made all the difference.

Congratulations, it's cancer

There's one more event from my high school years that to this day stands as the defining experience of my life. A few months before graduation from high school, I started developing severe abdominal pain. Through a series of doctors' visits I discovered that I had testicular cancer.

A few weeks before graduation I had surgery to remove the tumor, and returned to school after a few days; I did my darnedest to keep my mouth shut because I did not want attention drawn to me on this matter. My sister, on the other hand, was a social butterfly, and immediately went back to school and told all her friends because, of course, she was looking for support for herself. You know, her brother was just diagnosed with cancer. And of course, it spread like wildfire. So as much as I tried to keep to myself, everybody was coming to me asking a lot of questions, "What's going on? What's the story? Are you gonna be OK?" All I wanted to do was finish school, for crying out loud. I only had a few weeks left, and it was hard enough to focus on finals as it was.

So I was able to finish up school and graduate. I had plans to start college in the fall but a follow-up blood test a month later showed that the cancer had come back and was raging through my system and I was immediately rushed into chemotherapy. I spent the entire summer throwing up, losing my hair, losing my friends and losing my mind.

The friends I was in contact with stopped talking to me. I suspect they didn't know how to handle it and employed the "out of sight, out of mind" strategy. I learned many years later that the rest of them simply didn't know that the cancer had come back and were focused on moving forward with their own lives, college plan, etc. So I was basically left there in a desert of pain and uncertainty with little support.

It was the worst experience of my life while I was going through it. I had the hospital staff, and I had my family, who were scrambling to keep their heads on straight. We had a family business that my folks had to attend to. My mother was amazing in terms of doing her part for the business and making sure I was taken care of at the hospital. She needed to kick a little ass more than once. But for the most part, I had an almost nonexistent support system. My parents tried, but how do you support an eighteen-year-old with cancer?

Our church at the time was very inattentive. We would make an effort to reach out to them and the response was, "We'll pray for you" and nothing else. So through that period of my life—not knowing I was on the spectrum then—I experienced the sensory chaos that was caused by the side effects of the chemo. That was bad enough—to be nauseous and be in pain—but imagine that you have a very sensitive nervous system already.

Fortunately, as you can tell, that chapter of my life had a happy ending and continues to be a source of tremendous value for my life. I chronicled the entire experience in my book, *What To Do When You're Totally Screwed*. As I was to learn, having survived cancer was a tremendous asset in preparing me for the responsibilities I have today.

Chapter 2

I Made Myself
a Promise

All these years later I work full time consulting with parents, schools, and professionals on how to most effectively prepare the spectrumites in their lives for the world. I have been asked repeatedly by parents to teach their spectrum children how to have the self-awareness I do. When I explain that I learned it by necessity and how I learned it, they understand why my level of self-awareness is so deep and thorough. Unlike many spectrumites who have the luxury of avoiding their problems and becoming distracted by other activities, I was immersed in a reality so intense there was no avoiding it. I had indescribable physical pain in every inch of my body, and I was in and out of a cramped hospital room, where I was poked, prodded, and violated for the sake of curing my cancer.

I was throwing up constantly, all my hair fell out, and I had no say in the matter. I had no predictability. My doctors wouldn't give me straight answers to any of my questions, including whether I was going to live or die. I simply couldn't get my psychological or emotional needs met and I experienced levels of rage, panic, terror, depression, and every other emotion that most people don't experience in their worst nightmares. My experience was as deep and raw as humanly imaginable without driving someone insane. All of those places deep inside ourselves that people spend their days avoiding through denial and rationalization are the parts that were thrust into my awareness.

So when the day finally came that I was told my cancer was in remission and that I would live, I was faced with all of this raw emotion, mistrust, confusion, and no idea where to go or what to do next with this second chance at life.

I did make a decision though. I decided that I refused to live the rest of my life being miserable. Most importantly, I made myself a promise, that I would never be that helpless ever again. So I finally got to the point where I realized that no one could give me any answers on how to find peace or balance in the situation, so I had to figure it out for myself. I basically spent the next two years in and out of the local library. I read countless books on psychology and philosophy in search of the mental strategies I needed to pull myself together.

In order to honor my decision not to be miserable or helpless, I had to spend a lot of time in those deep, vulnerable places that everyone else avoids. Needless to say, I became a master of introspection and self-discovery. So while others choose to watch a TV show, or read a fantasy novel to escape themselves, I watch my own thinking—I watch how I respond to things and make the choices I do. If those thoughts lead to misery or helplessness, thoughts of "poor old me" or "I can't do it," then I ask myself, "How do I do better?"

I am determined not to allow myself to feel so terrified again. I don't mean that in the sense that I would deny my feelings—I wanted more tools, solutions, so if I was ever in a similar position, I could get out of it and be more resourceful.

It ultimately came down to what happened in my thinking. I'd lived in a bubble my whole life, like most people do: a bubble meaning the barrier between ourselves and everything else, a barrier created by the collection of beliefs and perceptions that we use to protect ourselves from the things we don't want to think about, including ourselves.

When you're in high school, when you're living with your parents, your needs are met. Think about how many problems of life are solved for us growing up. Most of them. You're being taken care of. Then all of a sudden I was bombarded with problems of trust, mortality, faith, some really heavy stuff. Trying to make sense of the fact that my friends didn't want to talk to me. My innocence had been absolutely ripped away from me in terms of what I thought life was, who I was, what life is about. With so little support, I was left to either lose my mind entirely, or find some kind of meaning to the situation.

So the book that I wrote was all about how I emerged from that complete state of chaos and helplessness to get my head in a place where I could live again and live with some degree of trust and direction and purpose. Through my work with the spectrum community, more people are discovering that book. Even though it wasn't written for the spectrum community, they're finding it extremely relevant to their own lives because, of course, it came from the mind of a spectrumite working hard to find structure and balance during chaos. It came from the spectrum mind even though it doesn't speak specifically to Asperger's.

Why college was almost an ending instead of a beginning

After I weathered that storm and found some direction in my life again, I started college. I took a few classes at my local community college and probably tried five different majors. It was during that time that I realized I still had a lot of anger and mistrust, which was really getting the better of me. I had difficulty sorting it out on my own and I realized I needed help.

My mom was able to connect me with a social worker. Looking back now, I consider the gentleman I worked with to have been a gift from God. It couldn't have been a better fit. I worked with him for about two years on the feelings of anger, betrayal, and trust. He had his work cut out for him but he was so patient and very wise. It was my work with him that inspired me to pursue social work as a major and as a profession.

After all I'd been through and how far I'd come, I imagined that there had to be other people out there who are on a difficult journey and could really benefit from somebody who had been through that process. I eventually transferred to a private university close to my home.

My mother encouraged me to live on campus but I chose to commute. I toured the dorms; they were noisy and I felt extremely claustrophobic. This was clearly my spectrum sensibility kicking in. I was thinking, why on earth would I want to live someplace that isn't my home, with a bunch of people that I really don't want to socialize with? In my view, you go to school to learn, you don't go there to socialize. I knew it wouldn't work for me.

I would go to school, do my classes, and get the heck out of there. There were a few classmates that warmed up to me a little bit. I had some friendships, mostly intellectual; we'd sit around and talk about the concepts that we were learning in class, and whenever we'd talk shop, I was fine. But whenever they'd want to get together as a group and go someplace, I would opt out.

Not cut out for social work

Unfortunately my being less than social led to criticism from my classmates, who felt that social workers should be more social. They would say I was unfriendly, arrogant, assuming that I wasn't socializing because I thought I was too good for them or something. Which was a bunch of baloney, of course.

This led to my being summoned to the Office of the Dean of the School of Social Work on several occasions. She repeatedly scolded me for the behavior which was alienating my peers. She shared complaints that I was saying things that offended people. I had no idea what the heck she was talking about. A few classmates had remarked that I was too blunt when responding to a request for my honest opinion. Back then my answers were completely unfiltered. I'd tell it like I saw it.

One of the main reasons this problem got out of hand is because they would routinely talk about me (with each other) instead of to me about how upset they were. Then they would complain to the dean.

So when the dean informed me of this, I was shocked because no one had said anything to me. Telling me I'm too blunt doesn't alert me to the fact that people felt alienated because of it. Her advice, of course, was that I should just stop it and be more social. This was incredibly disheartening because I was hearing this from a Ph.D. level social work instructor who wasn't interested in my perspective; she really wasn't interested in educating me about what I needed to do differently; she just told me to stop it.

I felt more and more alienated myself in that environment. I was told that being myself was unacceptable and that I was expected to be who they wanted me to be without any guidance. I was expected to "get it." The dean suggested on several occasions that I wasn't cut out to be a social worker and should switch majors. I became so miserable that I dropped out of college for close to five years.

I'm going to be a father

I was so conflicted because I really wanted to do social work but the whole time I was there I felt like the proverbial square peg being forced into a round hole. So I spent the next five years living at home, and floundered around from one job to the next trying to figure out what to do with my life.

It was during that time while working at a hospital that I met a petite, shy nurses' aide who was just as socially awkward as I was.

We fell in love quickly, and got married quickly within ten months and bought a very small place together. Within a few months of being married, we learned she was pregnant with Zachary.

Looking back now I'd say our relationship was driven more by impulse and immaturity than love. Finding out she was pregnant was a cause for celebration throughout the family, partially because of what I said earlier about being told I would probably never be able to have kids. It was also a serious wake-up call for me. I realized I needed to stop floundering around trying to find my way and make a decision. With a baby on the way, I needed to be able to contribute to my family in a more substantial way.

After a lot of soul searching and lengthy discussions with my wife, I realized that social work was still something that I was really compelled to follow through on. As fate would have it, in order to reenter the program I'd previously attended after almost five years, I would have to get the approval of the dean who thought I wasn't fit for the profession.

Sure I could have applied to other schools, which I did. But between distance, scheduling, and financing, the school I'd begun at was the best fit. So I prepared myself for the meeting with the dean. She and I had a sit-down, and I told her how far I'd come in the time since I'd left, how much I'd learned about myself, and how I fully intended on things being a vast improvement over my previous experience in the program.

What I'd basically done was silently resign myself to keeping my mouth shut and getting through the program without ruffling any feathers. I was going to speak only when spoken to. So the dean accepted me into the program where I finished my undergrad degree and began graduate school in the fall.

My spectrum mind gets to shine

It was in grad school that I started discovering some of the talents that I can attribute to being on the spectrum. These talents have turned out to be of tremendous value for my clients and the larger spectrum community.

It helped a great deal that grad school was taught primarily through lecture and dialogue, which fit with my auditory learning style so well that I was using my brain more fully than I ever had before in a classroom. All through grade school and afterwards, instruction had been primarily visual, reading, copying notes from the board and taking tests. All the ways I struggled to learn. I never got a chance to reach my potential because I was using my brain in the most inefficient way possible. So these newly discovered abilities never had a chance to reveal themselves in a noticeable way until now.

The first ability I discovered was my knack for "watching a person think," as I call it. When I listen to a person discuss their beliefs, opinions, and points of view, I can see their words line up similarly to assembling a puzzle. It's a form of pattern recognition that is strictly auditory. Pattern recognition in spectrumites is stereotypically thought of as visual such as remembering license plate numbers or other strings of facts that were experienced visually.

I didn't experience the world in that way. Now couple this ability with the years of introspecting and getting to know my own thought patterns, and now I had developed somewhat of a radar for picking up thinking patterns which I could identify and problem solve quickly.

Many spectrumites are systematic thinkers, meaning they understand how parts of a system interact with each other to make the system work. I've had a few clients who could read computer code like somebody else would read words in a book. I'm able to see human thought the same way. People think in a systematic way, in a pattern. So even if their thinking might be faulty and negative in some way, there's a pattern to it. So I listen for the pattern and am able to explain to the person how they create the experiences they do that result in the problems they're having. I can also tell them how to change it in order to create the results they want. Like a mechanic figuring out why your car is making that funny noise and what to do about it.

You may be wondering how I actually discovered this ability. Part of this ability allows me to hear every word a person says, whereas the average person (so I'm told) hears the overall theme of what another person says. So, when a topic was being discussed in class, the other students were listening in a more abstract way, listening for themes and meaning, and I was catching all the details. For example, we'd have to do role-plays to try out our clinical skills and receive feedback from our classmates. I'd listen intently to both the person in the role of the clinician and the classmate in the role of the client.

While the rest of the class listened for the themes and read between the lines, I caught the inaccuracies between what the client said and what the clinician repeated back to demonstrate that he or she was listening. I seemed to be the only one, apart from the teacher, who was catching this. Fortunately my classmates appreciated it and so did the teachers. My classmates actually began seeking me out because there were aspects of our learning that needed a detail-oriented mind, and I was an asset on group projects. It was incredibly validating to be appreciated in this way.

Another thing my systematic thinking allowed me to do was break things down into smaller pieces quickly, like complex concepts. In my mind, big ideas are like large public places, too big, too overwhelming, so I like them in smaller pieces that I can examine more closely.

So when the professor would explain a concept and the rest of the class looked at her confused, it got to the point where the teacher would say, "Brian, could you help me out here?" I would explain it in a more simplified way and everyone would say, "Ohhhhhh." So the teachers appreciated this ability as well.

It also seemed to be an ability no one else, including the teachers, had. They just didn't think the way I did, but they clearly had use for it. This is an ability that has been one of my greatest assets when working with spectrum clients because I'm able to explain social situations in a systematic way so they're easier to understand and navigate.

My first job as a social worker

Things really turned around for me in grad school. In fact, one of my best friends to this day is someone I met in grad school. About three months prior to graduation I applied for a social work position with a hospice agency and was hired. I felt my cancer history would help me relate to those experiencing serious illness. This was actually my first full-time job. Before that I worked on and off for my parents' business when they needed help. Either that or I worked for temp agencies. I really never had steady employment where I had to show up five days a week.

This was an adjustment in more ways than one. I also had to navigate a bureaucratic web of unspoken rules that I would break frequently. At times it felt like playing pin the tail on the donkey in a windstorm. My tendency to be very direct and do the logical thing got me into a whole lot of trouble. Many of my coworkers would cringe while watching me naively challenge the establishment. Some remarked that I was brave for doing so, but honestly, it was just social ignorance. I didn't know any better.

Fortunately I was good enough at my job that they were happy to have me. I left on my own terms when I learned my wife and I were expecting our third child. I went to work for a larger hospice and received a substantial increase in pay. Thank goodness, because we really needed it.

The new job was great at first because my supervisor was very kind and patient. The social workers I shadowed for the first few weeks were very supportive and accepted me right away. We became close as colleagues.

About a year later we got a new supervisor and everything went downhill. I found him to be unpredictable in his expectations and in his communication with me. It got to the point where I was dreading going to work. My heart would start racing every time my pager went off. He was constantly changing his mind about what he wanted me to do. My day rarely had any structure. It was a nightmare for a spectrumite.

My family in crisis

It was also during that time that my eldest, Zach, started first grade and all the news about Asperger's entered our lives. I was a nervous wreck. At work I had a supervisor I didn't get on with and at my son's school it seemed to me the staff were more interested in their rules and regulations than they were in doing anything meaningful for Zach.

I was being called to the school a few times a week because Zach was having meltdowns and running from the room. So I had to explain to my difficult supervisor why I was having to cut my workday short repeatedly to handle my son's issues.

The final straw was when the principal sat me down and suggested I have my son medicated in order to control his behavior. To cut a long story short, we pulled him from school and homeschooled him for almost two years.

I was driven during this time by my promise never to be helpless again, and I wasn't going to let my son suffer so I read more and more books and located a support group for parents with children on the spectrum. I had high hopes that the other parents would be filled with wisdom they could bestow upon me. But it wasn't the experience I expected. As I listened to the other parents talk about why they thought their kids did what they did and what they thought their kids were thinking, I knew from my own experience that they were way off. So I'd quickly say no, no, no, no, that's not what's going on. Then I'd explain to them what I felt their children were experiencing.

At first, they would just look at me with their jaws dropped and say, "Well, that makes so much sense." As much as I went there to get advice from them, before long, they began looking to me. The next thing I knew, each group would start with someone saying, "I want to ask Brian a question. I want to get Brian's thoughts on this." When they found out I was a social worker, they'd say, "Where's your office, can I bring my child to see you?" They assumed that I worked with these kids already.

I told them I was there trying to get help like they were. They kept urging me to see their children saying, "You don't understand, we'll pay you, we need your help with this. You know our child better than the person he's working with now." So after close to a year of being urged to do this, I found some inexpensive office space, put up a simple website, and opened my social work practice working with kids with Asperger's.

Another door opens

I started working a few evenings a week. I'd finish a long day at my hospice day job then see clients at my office. Word about my practice spread quickly, especially the novelty of an Aspie working with Aspies. Four months from the day I opened my office, my part-time therapy practice replaced my daytime income. That's how big the need was for what I had to offer; so I quit that day job and I haven't looked back since.

These days I'm doing a lot of writing and receiving more requests to do presentations all over the country, including school in-services. I've met some wonderful educators who really want the best tools for their students, and unfortunately I've met some who think they know it all and it's the students who need to do all the changing. All I can do is continue to share my ideas and strategies in the hope that at some point they'll wake up and realize that what they're doing isn't working and that they'll need to change, too.

Tragedy leads to opportunity

The sky seemed to be the limit at this point. Then, a few years ago, the mother of my three spectrum sons announced that she no longer wanted to be part of the family and she left us to be with another man. She became someone I didn't know and I found her a very difficult human being for a time.

I completely fell apart for months. My parents were extremely supportive and allowed me and the boys to move in with them while I got back on my feet. It was a rough period for all of us. I saw another social worker to handle the betrayal and collapse of my marriage. She was wonderful and helped me break through the feelings of helplessness in so many ways. My mother also pointed out to me that I had survived cancer and I could survive this. That, of course, reinforced my determination to keep the promise I'd made myself to never be helpless again. So I set myself a goal that my boys and I would be in our own house in a year.

Eleven months and three weeks later we moved into a rental home and began the next phase of our new lives. More and more I find myself in a place where I refuse to let life happen to me and am committed to creating the life my boys and I deserve.

As fate would have it, the grass-is-greener scenario my now ex-wife was pursuing went nowhere and she gradually worked her way back into her sons' lives. It has taken some time for her to regain their trust, but as of now, things look promising for her presence in their lives.

In this midst of all this upheaval and transformation, after nearly thirty years I reconnected with a childhood friend, my dear, sweet Cathy whom I mentioned earlier. We reconnected, as I said earlier, through a social networking site. We began talking on the phone, then we started hanging out, then hanging out more, and then we became inseparable.

When she met the boys, it was like they were already part of the same family. The connection she has with them is incredible and they are extremely close. Cathy is the best friend I've ever had and I've become more than I thought I could be with her in my life.

She truly appreciates my eccentricities, who I am as a person, and our personalities complement each other so well that we make each other better when we're together. We have our disagreements but are so dedicated to our relationship that we're committed to working through every difficulty. I learn so much from our relationship that it makes my work helping spectrumites understand relationships that much more powerful.

Chapter 3

It's All About Calm and Focus

I had an in-depth conversation with two young parents of an eight-year-old boy we'll call Charlie. They'd just learned he was on the spectrum and were trying to wrap their minds around the implications it had for their lives.

They began their search for answers on the internet as many people do. This resulted in even more confusion, as they were unable to find a consistent definition of autism they could understand. Explanations of autism ranged from it simply being a different way of seeing the world to being a debilitating neurobiological disease that needed to be cured. In all of their research they couldn't find anything that described Charlie, let alone how to help him.

I encouraged them to start by taking a deep breath and reminding themselves that the internet is a place where anyone with an opinion can post whatever they want and call it the truth. So if they wanted a reliable source for where to begin they needed to look no further than Charlie. Their job is to learn to understand his experience of being on the autism spectrum.

The characteristics of autism they recalled during our conversation were digestive problems, meltdowns, restricted interests, and difficulty making friends. They didn't recall reading anything about what it felt like to be on the spectrum, only examples of what you'd notice as an outside observer. The missing piece was what the person with autism is experiencing that results in what you see.

What it means for him

I asked them to consider the expression, "Don't judge a book by its cover." In Charlie's case and in getting to know others on the spectrum, it's critical that you don't get to know him by what you can observe alone. They must get to know Charlie's world as much as they can. Of course, neither of them are Charlie and neither of them have his experiences. Just like Tony (Charlie's father) doesn't know what it feels like to be Tina (Charlie's mother) and vice versa.

Though they may be very close and share a lot with each other, they agreed they don't know what it feels like to be on the inside of the other person looking out at the world.

What no article, book, or seminar could ever teach them is what it feels like to be Charlie. That is his experience and unique to him.

I told them that, "The way to begin helping him is by realizing that no degree of expertise on autism makes you an expert on Charlie. You can get to know Charlie and the things he's willing and able to share with you, the things he's willing to allow you to see, but the only person with all of the information, with all of the experience of what it's like to be Charlie is Charlie. So what this means for you is to get to know what Charlie's autism is like for him. The definitions of autism speak very generally. Charlie is very specific. Autism is like a fingerprint. We all have fingerprints but we each have our own. Autism is called a spectrum and can be thought of as a spectrum of neurological fingerprints. Does this make sense?"

I have learned to understand my autism fingerprint by studying my own nervous system. That means thinking about all of my experiences of interacting with the world. Even more important are my experiences about myself that come from my experiences with the world. It's important to be aware of how Charlie feels about himself because of the difficulty he has. Every experience he has can have a significant impact on how he sees himself and the amount of worth he feels he has. I and other spectrumites go through every moment of our lives actively trying to solve the problems of how to do this thing called life. Because of the unique challenges that come with being a spectrumite, we often have great difficulty solving the problems of how to feel good about ourselves when we're corrected more than we're complimented. How to understand what our needs are when we're often told what they're supposed to be instead of being helped to discover them for ourselves.

The toughest problem to solve is how to utilize other people. How the whole "we" thing works. That critical connection of partnership is the most illusive to spectrumites. The "we" goes beyond relationships with people; it also refers to the relationship with the environment you're in.

As the people and the environment around Charlie change, Charlie needs to assess those changes and adjust accordingly. According to Tony and Tina, if there's one thing Charlie doesn't like, it's change.

Change isn't the problem

Tina described Charlie as being stubborn. In my experience it isn't a matter of stubbornness. The reason spectrumites don't like change isn't because they want to have their way; they don't like change because their nervous systems have to work ten times harder to adjust to the change around them. That extra work can be exhausting and sometimes mentally and physically painful.

As I mentioned before, the autism spectrum is an experience. The way I define the autism spectrum is "the ongoing struggle to stay calm and focused with a globally disorganized nervous system." For Charlie, the disorganization presents as clumsiness in moving his body, and difficulty writing. He won't make eye contact when talking to someone, likes to be alone a lot, and he gets upset very easily.

That is because his entire nervous system is disorganized, but in a way that it unique to Charlie. It is his autism fingerprint. His nervous system has difficulty organizing movement, focus, and probably many other things. He becomes easily frustrated because he has to work so hard to organize his experience and make sense of it. But he's doing so with a nervous system that is disorganized. Does that make sense?

Keep in mind that all I've given you is an explanation. The actual experience of being that disorganized is more intense than you might imagine. I'll use myself as an example because I can speak about my own experiences. I have many sensory sensitivities, to touch, light, sound, motion, smell, you name it. When there is too much of any one sensory experience, I become disorganized even further. Because while I'm moving through the world trying to stay calm and focused (two states which are easier to achieve with an organized nervous system) my nervous system is inundated with sensory information that it has to organize while it's working like crazy to organize itself. Imagine how intense and disorienting that experience is.

Stimming is a must

Stimming is when someone rocks, flaps, fidgets, hums, and so on. When the information comes in a greater amount, intensity, or speed than my nervous system can handle, I can become overloaded. I may become more moody, and will begin using my body in interesting ways such as rocking or flapping, two things Charlie was observed doing as well. In my experience, the more disorganized I feel, the more I need to use my body or my mind in an organized way to help me organize my nervous system. I will either rock my feet at the ankles, or my body at the hips, and often I'll start looking for even numbered things to count because organized things around me help me feel more organized. Some professionals, in my opinion, mistake this for obsessive-compulsive disorder (OCD), when for many spectrumites it is a very strategic way to stay organized. Also commonly observed in spectrumites, including Charlie, is making a point of lining things up and stacking things. This is just like when a person gets up and stretches after sitting for too long, or takes a walk or a drink of water to give their body a little maintenance throughout the day in order to keep going. Spectrumites have the added work of needing to do things to stay organized on top of all the rest of the stuff other people do. Charlie routinely gets in trouble at school for getting out of his seat and for not paying attention.

Respecting his style

People have preferences towards certain learning styles, ways they learn best: visual, auditory, or kinesthetic. *Kinesthetic* refers to learning by moving your body. I have three boys on the autism spectrum who represent all three learning styles. One wants to talk all the time but not move much—he's more auditory. Another wants to watch movies and play video games—he's more visual. The last one has to be moving all the time, and that has translated well into getting him involved in chores around the house and helping in the kitchen. He's excited to do these things because it keeps him moving.

But then when he goes to school, they want him to sit still. He's extremely fidgety during circle time, the time in which they want him to sit on the floor scrunched together with other students and passively listen to the teacher read a story. When I asked the teacher to explain what being able to sit still and listen during circle time teaches him, she replied, "It prepares him for how to behave in the classroom."

What I then explained to her was that it may teach him to do what will serve the teacher and perhaps his fellow students, who need a quiet environment to learn, but I needed to know when his needs would be met. He needs to move in order to keep his nervous system organized. By following the rules of circle time, he's being taught that success in the classroom requires him to accept feeling disorganized.

Being disorganized makes it difficult for him to focus, learn, or even enjoy being at school. Does this make sense? I need to explain this to school personnel on behalf of clients quite often.

When Charlie's needs are met in the classroom, it will be easier for him to be there and he'll be easier to teach. The only way for the teachers to get what they need is for Charlie to get what he needs. Win–win is the only solution.

The nervous system of someone on the autism spectrum is disorganized by default, whereas the neurotypical or average person's nervous system is more coordinated; things work better together in order to accomplish things such as focusing, paying attention, and using your body in a coordinated way for walking, playing sports, and writing. The nervous system also needs to be organized to accomplish things such as making decisions, regulating your mood, maintaining a sleep schedule, and even digesting food. Some spectrum kids have digestive issues because their nervous system has difficulty digesting things in an organized way. I, for one, get horrendous stomach cramps and other digestive problems from drinking milk. I use rice milk instead, and it's made a huge difference.

So, as I told Charlie's parents, when Charlie is rocking or humming, we should think of these as strategies he uses to keep himself organized. In the absence of these things, he feels much more disorganized and therefore less able to feel calm and focused. It isn't a matter of teaching Charlie how to feel calm and focused. He does it already. It's more a matter of helping him understand that this is the benefit of his rocking, flapping, etc.

I told Tony and Tina, "Over time you can help build his self-awareness around what works best for him. For now, I'd like to explain more about what's at the heart of the experience of feeling disorganized. The better you understand it, the better you can guide him. For the most part, spectrumites take a hit-or-miss approach to life in terms of finding what works. After all, how many other people with disorganized nervous systems do they have as role models for how to make the world work? Often none. The ones trying to help don't know what it's like for him so they have difficulty helping him correctly.

"They mean well, but they don't know as much as they could in order to help him more effectively. That's why we're having this conversation. The more you learn, the better you can help Charlie learn. Then together you can educate all who need to be able to work with Charlie to help him succeed. In the end, Charlie will learn to do this for himself as his own best advocate. That's the ideal outcome."

Finding focus

Now let's understand what focus is. It is more than simply paying attention. Let's think of it not only in terms of attention but also in terms of sustaining that attention. For the average person, giving something your attention is automatic. For a spectrumite, it is a deliberate act. Then keeping that attention is even more difficult. Are you familiar with the term *hyperfocus*? *Hyperfocus* is focusing on something so completely that your mind doesn't take in any information that's irrelevant to what you're focusing on. When my second eldest brother would watch TV as a child, he'd be so focused that if someone was talking to him or a very loud noise happened, he wouldn't even flinch. Because when hyperfocused, his brain tuned out everything around him. The main downside is that being suddenly jarred from a state of hyperfocus can be psychologically painful and extremely disorienting because your brain has to shift so fast.

Tina described how angry Charlie gets when she turns off the TV because he isn't listening. She called herself an idiot after learning what that did to him. I reassured her that she simply had no idea. Now that she knew different, she could do different. That is intelligence.

I told her, "Now that you know different you also need to understand that when spectrumites feel calm and focused, that's when we're organized. What would you say are opposites of calm and focused: hyper and scattered perhaps? It can also mean feeling restless all the time, tired because of all the work trying to stay focused. The responsibility of a spectrumite is to learn what helps him to be calm and focused, what prevents it, sabotages it, and how to get it back when he starts to lose it. We'll discuss how this is accomplished in future conversations."

Most parents, teachers, etc., don't understand the need for calm and focus, and the spectrumites themselves stumble upon what works but don't know why and how, and are unable to communicate it to those around them. I've had clients whose parents were upset because they spent all day reading a book, watching movies, and sometimes playing the same scene over and over again. My eldest son ruined many a DVD doing this when he was younger. Now we digitally download our movies to prevent this. The most common concern I hear is excessive video game playing.

Now for the spectrumite, these activities are preferred because they increase the experience of calm and focus. They increase it in a way that is easier to accomplish, more accessible, and therefore more enticing as a way to feel good and also to avoid the things that are disorganizing.

From the outside, parents or teachers who don't know any better look and see a lazy child who is avoiding responsibility and avoiding people. Their solution is typically, "Stop it! Go do something else, go outside and play. Go meet people, ask someone to play." Charlie gets mad at Tina when she says things like that and responds with statements such as, "Leave me alone" or "I hate you."

Losing focus

For Tina, it's admittedly tough to hear statements like that. She feels he's being mean when she's only trying to help. She's concerned that he's missing out by not getting out there and interacting with other kids. Her intentions are in the right place but I explained to her that behind the words "I hate you" are the fears of the pain he'll experience if he does what she's asking him to do. She's asking him to give up doing what he knows will organize him, and go into a situation that he cannot control or predict, and may not even know how to stay calm and focused in. So he probably hears her repeated requests to do something else as unsupportive.

Of course she couldn't know this because as a social being it's counterintuitive for her. Even more problematic is that Charlie probably doesn't know either so he's unable to understand or explain why her requests are so frustrating. So what chance do parents have when they don't understand and neither does their child? The chance they have begins with asking for help from people like myself and other spectrumites who have learned it and can guide them.

Charlie's resistance to do other activities besides the ones that organize him goes beyond the unpredictable nature of the activity. It is also about the skills required to be effective in that activity. Being social, especially with more than one person at a time, requires multitasking. You need to pay attention to more than one thing at a time and keep track of those things. Would you agree? Spectrumites are unitaskers; we are not multitaskers. This means we are at our best when focusing on one thing at a time and not many things at once.

Unfortunately, we are usually asked to be at our best in a multisensory, multitasking environment like a classroom, public place, or workplace. Things that are distracting to us surround us and prevent us from focusing, and we are then criticized for not focusing. This can be torture at times.

Classroom contradictions

Now imagine this: a unitasking spectrumite is in a classroom and has to choose one thing to pay attention to. The teacher wants to be it. When we do want to pay attention to the teacher, we have difficulty deciding what to pay attention to. Do we pay attention to what she's saying, what she's doing, or what she's writing? We try to focus on what works best for us. The challenge is when the teacher doesn't do enough talking, writing, showing, or whatever that one way we learn best is. We end up getting maybe ten percent of what was taught in any given class, then we're scolded for not paying attention in class, being lazy, unmotivated, you name it.

My prevailing message to all teachers is that you can't ask for what you aren't willing or able to give. Don't expect a student to learn if you aren't willing or able to teach the way the student needs to be taught. Don't ask a student for flexibility if you're stubborn. Don't keep encouraging a student to ask for help if you're going to turn them away when they do. Most importantly, don't assume that your experience is the norm. Don't minimize or criticize a child who isn't doing something you want, the way you want, as fast as you want. Instead, work to learn what makes it difficult for a child to rise to the level of expectation and then meet the child halfway as often as needed.

Now I want to make one thing very clear. I have met many teachers who are eager to do everything mentioned above. They are also, however, met with increasing class sizes, workloads, "one size fits all" government mandates, and administrators who are sometimes more interested in being right than being effective. In the US the mandates I'm referring to are well-known state and federal testing standards. Even in their absence, the mind-set of our school system is an emphasis on grades above all else. This is evidenced by the myriad of times school staff have ignored the low self-esteem and social exclusion of a child by stating, "But his grades are good so he's doing well." These same teachers also have to deal with parents who demand they meet all of their spectrumite's needs and make other children play with their child, and then chastise staff for less than perfect outcomes, all the while doing little if anything on their end. I've encountered these scenarios far too often and everyone loses, especially the child.

One of the most common problems in working within bureaucratic institutions is if you're there long enough the limits and inflexibility of the institution can infect your thinking, which in turn becomes limited as well.

In some cases there is an element of hypocrisy. They expect spectrumites to do everything their way and then accuse spectrumites of the same expectation when spectrumites don't comply. This is the classic win–lose, "my way or the highway," approach. You must seek the middle ground where both people do some work. Which includes doing some bending yourself.

Tina asked how to begin teaching Charlie this approach when he is so inflexible. I explained to her that spectrumites navigate the world deliberately, not automatically. Everything can be an exhausting act of will. Flexibility in thinking requires the ability to shift gears automatically and quickly. The spectrum brain doesn't do that; it needs to choose to change and then do it, two steps, and conscious steps, not one automatic step. Imagine how exhausting it is to have to change, change, then change again. Does it make sense that you'd want to stay the same as much as possible because of the work it takes to change?

The reality, of course, is that life requires change. But it doesn't require that one person do all the changing. The majority of the change that causes spectrumites the greatest amount of frustration is the change demanded by other people without any negotiation.

Keeping it together

Now keep in mind that as the autism spectrum is on a continuum, so are its characteristics, including flexibility. You can think of the autism spectrum as a continuum of disorganizational challenges or challenges in staying organized.

It seems to me that the more difficult it is for a child to organize their nervous system, the more autistic that child is. Some spectrumites have speech delays or are unable to verbalize. Some are quick to become overloaded and have a meltdown, while others appear to be more resilient. It all comes down to how hard that child has to work to stay organized, calm, or focused, while also being required to organize the information around them. The harder it is to stay organized, the easier it is to become more disorganized by the outside world or even changes within yourself such as going from a state of boredom to excitement. That change needs to be regulated, too.

A child who is more autistic may need to give his undivided attention to maintaining his own internal organization. Then someone comes along and wants to talk to him. He may become angry because it's difficult to focus on maintaining his own organization while also organizing the experience of talking to the other person. This is the spectrumite who is often referred to as living in his own world. His world takes a lot of work to maintain, which makes it extremely difficult at times to include yours.

Let's talk a little about how stimming (rocking, flapping, fidgeting, humming, and so on) helps maintain organization. One of my sons makes noises when he's excited, noises that others find upsetting. These noises help him stay organized when he becomes excited quickly by releasing some of the increased energy. Hand flapping serves this purpose as well. (I flap when I get excited while watching movies or when I hear exciting news.) While I respect that the noises or flapping can be disruptive to others at times, simply telling him not to do them is unreasonable. Because what others refer to as disruptive behavior is actually very functional for my son. While they may cause problems for others, they are solutions for him. They solve the problem of disorganization.

I have experienced that others find it difficult to understand that even positive emotions can be disorganizing. Even though they're positive, they are also intense and require regulating. As I've said, spectrumite nervous systems don't self-regulate effectively so we give it a little help by stimming.

Finding his way

I asked Tony to describe some of the things he wishes he was better at doing, those things many of us try to do repeatedly but just can't seem to make work. He explained that he had never been particularly good at sports. His brother was the athlete in the family, and Tony had trouble even throwing a ball straight. Tony and I have that in common. In fact, Tony's family was sports oriented which alienated him in many ways from them due to athletics not being a strength of his.

Tony developed beliefs about himself being weak, a wimp, and a loser. It was very hard for him to grow up in a family where he was criticized for not being who those around him envisioned themselves to be and wanted him to be as well. As Tony became an adult he began to feel differently about himself. This shift began when he found something he was better at than others around him, repairing cars. He's so good in fact that he is the most requested mechanic at the shop that employs him. So now, when it comes to whether he can play sports or not he could care less.

I explained to Tony that we're all wired to do different things and that sports aren't something his nervous system is organized to do. Some people are organized to throw curve balls, others to cook magnificent meals; some are organized with encyclopedic memories but the inability to speak.

As his parents get to know Charlie, they're also learning his strengths and what his nervous system is organized to do, as well as his challenges and what his nervous system isn't organized to do at all or without help.

Again, we're talking about his unique autism fingerprint, his specific combination of strengths and challenges, or organization and disorganization. So in Tony's case, throwing a pitch is not something that his brain and body are wired to organize doing. But fixing cars is.

I know people who can look through their cabinets, know everything they need to buy, go to the store without a list, and remember everything. I happen to need a list. The list is an accommodation that helps me organize, because my brain does not organize effectively around that activity. In time, I told his parents, we will help Charlie find his way as well. We'll start by helping him find his calm and focus.

Chapter 4

It Takes Strength to Connect with You

Anna came to see me about her ten-year-old son Trevor. She was concerned by how difficult it was for Trevor to stay focused during a conversation. She described it as spacing out and wanted guidance in helping him to manage it so she could communicate with him better.

I asked Anna how she reengages Trevor when he spaces out. Her response was to ask if he was listening and she was adamant that he should look at her when she talks to him and make eye contact. I asked why she requested eye contact from Trevor. "Because that's how I know he's paying attention to me," she replied. The following are the critical points from our discussion.

Is it possible to look a person in the eye and not be paying attention? Of course it is. With that established, I will explain why Trevor has such a difficult time staying engaged when talking to Anna. The neurotypical (average person's) mind is wired to connect automatically, effortlessly and without thought. No amount of social skills classes, books read, or hours of behavioral therapies will change the following fact. For spectrumites, the very act of connecting with another person is a deliberate, conscious act that requires sustained mental effort. Though I have shared this fact with many, who then claim to understand, their actions prove otherwise. Clearly, they understand the idea but not the experience.

Connecting by choice

This goes much deeper than simple difficulty paying attention. Trevor has to choose to pay attention, to connect with you. I'm not using the word *choice* as in "preference." It isn't choice in the sense that he could do it if he wanted to and simply chooses not to. His brain doesn't automatically tune in simply because he's being spoken to. His brain doesn't automically tune in or tune out. For spectrumites, attention and connection require the same deliberate effort and decision as standing up or taking a step. It won't happen unless you intend that action first and then concentrate to execute that action.

It really is that difficult. Keep in mind, the effort I just described is what's required to give a person or an activity your *initial* attention. Now if you want our undivided or sustained attention, then it gets very complicated. Being required to consciously sustain connection is like asking someone to stand on one leg, for a long time, without losing balance and falling over. I would even venture to say that where a person lies on the autism spectrum can be measured, in part, by how much effort he has to put into the act of establishing and maintaining a connection. Connection, after all, is extremely difficult to maintain if you have a disorganized nervous system.

Why is it so hard for him to do? Well, why is it so hard for a blind person to see, or a deaf person to hear? It's because the nervous system either isn't wired to do it at all, or isn't wired to do it efficiently. In short, he isn't programmed for it. People who are wired to connect easily as you are don't realize that you do so automatically. This is crucial in understanding the spectrum mind in general. For the neurotypical mind, which is hardwired with the ability to automatically connect with others, this is an experience so natural that neurotypicals can't conceive of it being a difficult thing to do.

Connection is exhausting

Now consider that paying attention—connection—is required for more than just communication with other people. I would even say that connection, in any form, takes effort for spectrumites: connecting with a person, place, or thing, takes mental effort, and the more effort required, the more tired we become. The more things in the environment that require our attention, the more things we need to connect with, the more energy that must be expended, the more quickly we become exhausted.

Trevor expresses tremendous anxiety over the suggestion of having to go into crowded places or play on the playground when there are a lot of other children there. He doesn't like his social skills group either. Anna thought he was just being stubborn. I shared with her that, to this day, I avoid crowded places as well unless it is absolutely necessary.

Spectrumites have a hard time multitasking. For schoolchildren, eating in the cafeteria or going to parties can be disorienting and overloading. Social skills trainings may equip a spectrumite with the techniques for having a conversation, but it cannot equip them with the mental strength to make and sustain the connection their brain isn't wired to do.

Anna started feeling guilty for making Trevor do all these things. I encouraged her to be easy on herself and realize that she was acting on what makes sense to her. She was also acting on what other well-meaning but largely misinformed people were encouraging her to do.

One of Trevor's primary areas of difficulty is in school. If a spectrumite is routinely tuning out in class, it is because the mental effort required to connect is too much. Spacing out is a way of letting go of a connection that is too hard to maintain. Think of it as trying to hold on to a weight so heavy that your hands keep getting tired, until you finally have to let go. Only when your hands are rested can you pick it back up. No amount of saying, "Pick it up" or "Stay on task" will change that fact.

Now, imagine that you are being asked to hold something heavy on each finger—that is the experience of multitasking. That is what's required when listening, making eye contact, and watching body language at the same time. Asking this of spectrumites is psychological torture and socially selfish of anyone who requires it as a condition for being in a relationship with one of us.

Being aware

So how is he supposed to relate to other people if he's unable to do all that? How are other people supposed to know this about him? Education, that's how. Teach Trevor about himself so that he can confidently educate others about what he needs in order to give them what they need.

How do you teach him? With each and every interaction you have with him. It is a lot of work at first because it requires you to be more conscious of what you typically do automatically. Imagine how hard it is for a spectrumite to have relationships when the expectation is that he or she will make eye contact and pay attention until the other person has finished speaking. All while accounting for the thousands of nonverbal bits of information being transmitted during that time that is multitasking hell.

Imagine how much more quickly a spectrumite will get tired because of the mental effort to connect, as well as having to connect in multiple ways, and then maintain those connections. I would say that meltdowns, especially in public places, are in part the result of intense "brain fry." Add to this being tired or sick, and you'll have even less strength to make connections.

The high-functioning myth

How is he ever going to make it in this world? The same way any other person does. Together. The trick is that "together" needs to be redefined to allow for the unique way the spectrum mind does things. Let me explain further.

First, there's an important clarification I need to make. There's a term I continue to find upsetting, and it's a term often used to refer to me. The term is "high-functioning." It minimizes my challenges and those of anyone else to whom it is applied. A more accurate description would be "hides it better." What people perceive and irresponsibly refer to as "high-functioning" is (at least in my case) nothing more than intense, razor-sharp concentration on whatever I choose to focus on. When I am able to do it, the longer I do it, the more time I need to recover.

For example, when I present a five-hour seminar, it typically takes me about three to five days to fully recover. I don't shut down the whole time but I have to cut back my schedule so I can regain my strength and feel like myself again. Why do I do it then? It's far too important not to. I feel a sense of responsibility to do my part to create the changes we all need if we are going to learn to work together. It's too easy to sit back, complain, make excuses, and blame others for the way things are. Those are values I'd be ashamed to model for my boys.

I also feel humbled and honored to be able to make my contribution and have it valued by so many. It has taken more work than I can possibly describe. Some days I go to bed practically in tears from exhaustion. How do I keep going? I have managed to surround myself with some amazing people who help me a great deal in managing the more difficult areas of my life so I can do the things I need to do.

Day to day

Many people say I'm lucky to have such people around me. It isn't luck. These people are in my life because we have relationships that benefit each other. Relationships we've decided to have. I'll explain more about how I've accomplished this as we go on. Now let's talk more about how difficult it is for other spectrumites to manage their daily lives when connection is demanded of them by so many.

What it's like for me after presenting a seminar is what it can be like for a child attending school each day or an adult going to a busy workplace each day. When committing this level of concentration to repeated social connection, it is incredibly exhausting. When I've explained this to some people, they have naively suggested that I try not to concentrate so hard. But if you recall what I explained earlier about connection being like hanging on to a weight, when it comes to connection, you either hang on or let go.

For the all-or-nothing mind of a spectrumite, it isn't a matter of degree. You either fully "tune in" or you "tune out." I have learned to structure my life very strategically to avoid constant overload and burnout. I keep face-to-face human contact to a minimum because that requires the most strength for me; it requires the most strength to connect. My clients and my family get the most face time. I also avoid the phone, but e-mails and texts when short and to the point require far less effort to connect and are my preferred way of communicating. Trevor prefers chatting online with his friends to hanging out with them.

Some days, I don't even have the strength to connect online, so I avoid people altogether and become upset when people insist on connection. But I have a family so that isn't always possible. After an entire day of work, I sometimes need to go to my room to rest because I don't have the strength to connect either at all or to the degree my family requires. I need to rest first. Fortunately my wife is very understanding.

You will see this with spectrum kids who will come home from school exhausted from exerting tremendous strength to connect all day long, and their parents wonder why they'd rather tune out than talk. It's because they need to spend time disconnected in order to rest; their parents need to let them regain their strength to connect before engaging them.

Whether it's a child returning from school or an adult returning from work, recovering from a multisensory environment takes time. Being required to multitask is only part of the effort we must make. The other part is the effort we must expend to tune things out, in order to take in the things of interest.

Tune in or tune out

As spectrumites, our brains don't selectively ignore things. We must make simultaneous efforts to disconnect from some things, in order to connect with others. Try that in a cafeteria or a noisy workplace and see how long you last.

People, in general, don't realize that spectrumites experience everything around them simultaneously. It all comes in. The ability to multitask allows those who can multitask to prioritize some things and ignore others.

Spectrumites are unitaskers, one thing at a time. Therefore, we don't prioritize one sound over another sound. We experience all the sounds as a unified whole. So if there's a lot of sound, either in volume or variety, it can take its toll quickly. Teaching using a multisensory method (lecture plus overheads and handouts) is often confusing to someone who learns primarily through a single sense—visually, auditorily, or tactilely.

Even though we're inclined to "tune in" to the information entering through the preferred sense, we're simultaneously working to "tune out" the information coming into the nonpreferred sense. At least twice the effort is being expended to learn because, as I said before, the spectrumite brain tends to experience all of it ("tune in") or none of it ("tune out").

A quiet room with no distractions allows us to use our strength to connect ("tune in") because we don't have to also work to disconnect ("tune out"). As I observe people socializing, especially spectrumites, they gravitate toward the method and environment that works for them. I challenge any neurotypical to prove to me that, when they get together with their friends, they seek out the most chaotic environment, with the maximum number of distractions, in order to maximize their quality time together. Of course they wouldn't do that, and neither will spectrumites, because it would require too much effort to have that conversation in such an environment.

If you want to give spectrumites an opportunity to socialize, why then show them the profound disrespect of placing them in an environment that makes it even harder to do? It's like asking a runner to race, but on one leg, and then criticizing him when he tires quickly.

Accommodate instead of tolerate

The alternative to socializing in overloading environments isn't to allow a spectrumite to spend their lives in isolation. The solution is to teach those like Trevor to negotiate how they'll engage the world. Let me give you an example. One of my middle-school-aged clients had a predicament. He couldn't stand being in the cafeteria because it was too loud. He also didn't want to eat elsewhere because then his peers would start asking questions as to why. The problem was made worse when the school refused to let him use his music player and headphones, which would allow him to "tune in" to his music instead of expending the energy to "tune out" the chaos of the cafeteria. The result was that the effort he put into "tuning out" was so exhausting he would leave the lunch period, irritable, defensive, and often miserable. Classmates found it easier to upset him and took advantage of that fact. School was a horrible experience for him when he and I began working together.

Historically, the reaction of school staff was to treat his irritability as a behavioral issue and shame him for his behavior, and encourage him to learn better coping skills, to learn to tolerate the cafeteria. This was unhelpful behavior on their part as far as I'm concerned. How can you expect spectrum children to will their nervous system to withstand overload? You can't, it's completely unreasonable.

When this young man's parents involved me, I worked with him to discover the issues he was having with the cafeteria and how it affected the rest of his day. I then helped the school staff to understand this and to see how accommodation would solve the problems for him as well as reduce the disruptions in class from his resulting irritability. So they allowed him to use the headphones.

Wanting to connect isn't enough

I'm working diligently to encourage spectrumites and neurotypicals alike to make a wholehearted effort to understand why making a connection which can be invigorating for neurotypicals can be incredibly difficult and exhausting for spectrumites.

Even the people I enjoy being around often fail to realize that I must have the strength to connect with them. Simply wanting to socialize isn't enough if I don't have the strength at the time to make and maintain the connection with them.

In fact, this is why so many spectrumites prefer parallel play. Parallel play is when you're sitting with someone, maybe watching TV, playing video games, etc., but you aren't interacting with them. Parallel play allows us the privilege of enjoying the presence of another human being without the pressure for concentrated connection. It takes so much strength to socialize. This is why I keep my social circle small and my conversations brief. If you, for example, insist on chitchatting with me, you are requiring me to maintain my mental effort and concentration, while I wait for you to get to the point, with no clear sense of when you'll do so. You are asking me to hold on to a heavy weight that I'm not allowed to let go of until you've made your point. When I can no longer hold on and either look away or "tune out," you might call me rude or say, "Look at me when I talk to you."

Spectrumites need others to understand that we want to give you our attention. We also need you to understand what it takes for us to do so. The strength to connect is great. So please, value the time we are connected and the effort required to connect. Keep it short, sweet, and to the point. Even those little moments can be profoundly meaningful. Spectrumites, including myself, are more eager to interact with those they know will respect them and not be a source of exhaustion to interact with.

Knowing isn't understanding

Another thing that isn't understood well enough by either spectrumites, or those who work with them, is that spectrumites have disorganized nervous systems that must organize all of the sensory information inside and outside them all day long in order to navigate the world. They mistakenly believe that understanding it conceptually gives them an understanding of the experience. That would be like me claiming that I know what it's like to give birth to a baby simply because I've read about it. People with an organized nervous system simply cannot, and must not, fool themselves into believing that they understand the enormity of this experience.

What they must understand is that day after day, a person who does have this experience is worn down and typically without sufficient time to recover. Might this person who is worn down all the time feel tired, depressed, defeated, like he can't keep up? What kind of support does he get? He's told he's lazy, unmotivated, and needs to learn to cope better, when the reality is that he's worn out. Realizing you don't understand what it's like is an incredible gift to this conversation. When you understand that you don't understand, you are more willing and able to learn.

Chapter 5

My Senses Don't Play Well with Others, Including Me

I'm often asked by parents and professionals to lend insight into my sensory sensitivities. The hope is that they'll be better equipped to accommodate the sensory needs of the spectrumites in their lives so they can more effectively engage the world. In one particular presentation, all I needed to do was talk about what it was like getting there and being there.

The sensory migraine

I drove there on a busy highway, with cars driving past me at different speeds, changing lanes, etc. Then when I got there, I got out of an air-conditioned car into the hot outdoors, then entered an air-conditioned building and was cool again. That transition from cool to hot to cool was disorienting because my body had to make that quick shift and adjust to the fast and significant change in temperature. I literally become light-headed until my nervous system adjusts to the change and feels more organized. That doesn't happen quickly.

Once inside the building, I had to walk down a long hallway leading to the room I would present in. The carpet on the floor has a complex pattern that was visually overwhelming. So as I was trying to walk the long hallway and maintain my balance because of a combination of gross motor clumsiness and poor vestibular regulation, which makes me motion sensitive, I also had this pattern on the floor which increased the sense of motion because of all the visual information that moved as I moved. It's similar to driving past a row of trees.

Keep in mind that this experience isn't unique to this building. From the time I wake up until the time I go to sleep at night, I am constantly bombarded by sensory information that my brain does not coordinate very effectively. It is exhausting because of the extra stress on my nervous system that works, perhaps, ten times harder just to be in the world than the average person. For a person with classic autism it is probably fifty times harder.

The best way I could describe the experience of driving on the highway, changing lanes, being passed by big trucks, small trucks, fast, slow, all that inconsistency through my peripheral vision, going under bridges where there are sounds of trains and traffic overhead, lights flickering from various directions, is as a multitasking sensory migraine, and that would be the same experience going into a mall, going into a busy movie theater, or going into a conference, and that's pretty much my everyday experience. Is it a wonder many spectrumites don't want to leave the house?

I have a tremendous amount of respect for occupational therapists who work very hard to help spectrumites learn strategies to regulate their nervous systems when they're in environments like these. What can make their work more difficult is when younger kids on the spectrum don't know the OT is trying to help them.

All three of my sons on the spectrum receive occupational therapy, and one of the keys is to help them understand how your work solves a problem for them personally. Many young clients I work with have come to sessions already tired from what they've endured that day. If they come to sessions with an OT under similar circumstances it's harder to engage them and the work is more likely to be a source of frustration than of help. Many OTs, and other professionals for that matter, don't teach the parents how to prepare the child for their time working together.

One OT I've had the privilege of working with lets the kids play a little beforehand. They naturally find the activity that organizes them. Some like to swing, some like the weighted blanket, and when they feel more organized, it's much easier to engage them and do the work together. (A weighted blanket is made of heavier material to provide deep pressure over the entire body or a portion of the body. The common result is a calming effect for the user.) As I mentioned, getting to the room to present was a multitasking sensory migraine. So to help you get an idea of how many senses spectrumites need to multitask, or integrate, or account for at any given time, let me ask you a question. How many senses do we have?

How many senses do we have?

The common response to the previous question is five. Those five are sight, taste, hearing, touch, and smell. I like to think that there are actually five more that people aren't aware of, except for OTs. The sixth sense is vestibular, which is responsible for balance. It is controlled in your middle ear and detects motion based on the movement of your head.

Proprioception is next and is detected through nerves in your muscles and joints. These nerves are responsible for your brain's ability to determine where your body is in space. Whether you're standing, sitting, and so on. The remaining senses we'll discuss shortly.

Getting your needs met

A quick example of a child who is seeking vestibular input is a child who enjoys swinging or rocking. A child who likes to bang and crash (a slang term for rough play) and likes a lot of deep pressure is seeking more proprioceptive input in order to organize his nervous system.

My boys are such bangers and crashers I'm surprised I don't get a weekly call from child protective services because of all the bruises on their bodies. They like to somersault. They like to jump off the couch. They like to do flips on the couch. They like to slam into each other. They like to slam into the floor.

My five-year-old likes to jump up and slam his knees and shins into the floor, and he smiles when he does it. My joints creak getting off the couch. So he and I have very dissimilar experiences. But all the while, they're doing this to give their nervous system the input it needs to stay organized. Do you know a spectrumite who is always on the go and always seem agitated and can't sit down? What are your thoughts about this person's sensory needs? Basically, she's disorganized, and sitting still doesn't provide enough input to feel organized. In order to focus on anything, you need to be organized—integrated. A child who is not integrated has a lot of restless energy but nowhere to direct it, and ends up becoming very fidgety in an effort to keep that input coming in while meeting the expectation of sitting still in a classroom. She's always playing with this or messing with that, or messing with her brother's hair, or teasing her sister, or messing with this toy. Have you seen this?

If you have a child in preschool or kindergarten you will see much of this restlessness during circle time or any group listening activity. Sitting still quietly doesn't provide the necessary input for her to organize herself so she does what she must and fidgets to feel organized.

What's your frequency?

A teacher explained to me that group listening activities prepare students for further school life because they have to sit in a classroom and learn lessons for twenty or thirty minutes at a time and learn not to get up. They learn in five- or ten-minute increments because later on in school, especially when they get to high school, they'll have an hour-long period during which they'll be required to sit still. This sitting still exercise is supposed to hone that ability.

Though this is an important ability for the classroom, and works with children for whom sitting still isn't an issue, it doesn't do anything to help children on the spectrum learn to meet their sensory needs.

What if your child is a kinesthetic learner? A kinesthetic learner is somebody who has body wisdom: the carpenters, the people who are dancers, the ones who use their body as a primary way of engaging the world. If she needs to learn through her body, then sitting in a classroom for a ridiculous amount of time, being expected to learn through every sense except her body (proprioceptive and vestibular), then how successful is she likely to be?

The kids who bang and crash like my five-year-old need to use their bodies to regulate their nervous systems. These are the kids who, if allowed to pace in the back of the classroom, will absorb a great deal more information than they ever would sitting still. Of course, this isn't allowed; it's considered disruptive because it's not in service of the controlled environment that the public school system wants.

Now, since we're talking about learning styles, which refers to learning primarily through your body, your ears, or through your eyes, I want to share something that happened to me earlier this week. I am a predominantly auditory learner. I did a presentation and had several interactions with a gentleman responsible for making sure the microphones were working properly. I saw him earlier today providing the same service here, and I barely recognized him when he approached me because I don't remember faces very well, but I do remember voices and the unique way a person speaks. When I meet people in busy places such as this or at conferences, I read nametags to help me remember who people are in case I encounter them again. That is also why I don't use visual media in my presentations because it actually distracts and disorganizes me.

On the other hand, my wife, who's also on the spectrum, is very visual. When we go out together, it's wonderful. I'll share my experiences by saying, "Did you hear that?" And she'll say, "Ah, look at that." It's like we're on different radio frequencies, but when we get together, we help each other experience our environment more completely.

We took a trip to Manhattan a few months ago. I was listening to the noise, the taxis, everything else, and she was looking at the architecture. She was looking at architecture ten stories up and saying, "Oh, look, that's a gargoyle." She saw the detail. She's drawn to that. So it's wonderful having that combination because she can fill in a lot of the gaps in the environment that I miss. Otherwise, if there are a lot of visual things that I need to take in, I won't.

When I was in school, when a teacher used overheads or wrote things on the board to teach, she would lose my attention. When I did poorly in class, I would be told, "Well, you're not trying hard enough. You're not motivated enough." Simply because I wasn't getting the results they wanted me to get, learning via the method they felt like teaching. They didn't teach on my frequency. What did I do best? English class, language, poetry.

What's the intensity?

I wear shoes that have very thick heels because they have springs that are about two or three inches high. My body is so hypersensitive that when I walk—when my heel hits the ground— it feels like I'm stomping even though it's a regular step. I feel it all the way up into my head. So walking for any amount of time or distance gets exhausting very quickly because the feeling of walking is too intense. When walking around the house without my shoes, I often walk on my toes. Having these springs in my heels makes it so much easier to endure.

Now let's discuss the remaining senses. The remaining three are all in the skin: temperature, pressure, and pain. Now let's say all of these senses are hypersensitive, which means that what you would experience as typical, I would experience with much greater intensity. As I mentioned earlier, coming from the parking lot and entering this building required a transition from hot to cold. I'm temperature sensitive, so I felt that transition. Some people might say, "Oh, thank goodness it's cold." I think, "OK, give me a minute. I need to adjust. I need to settle in here."

So imagine a child who has temperature sensitivity, who goes from an air-conditioned house, to a hot school bus, to an air-conditioned school, and you wonder why he's fidgety and edgy. Then you want him to sit down, get his stuff out, get ready for class, stay on task, and his nervous system isn't even organized yet. But if a child doesn't know this about himself and can't communicate it, what happens to him typically? What is the feedback he gets from educators who want him to just sit down, be still, and cooperate? He's reprimanded for being off task. He's told to pay attention repeatedly. He's made to feel bad for something he hasn't the awareness, the time, or the strategies to remedy.

The bottom line is: his nervous system is what it is. It's disregulated. That's the nature of the spectrum, his ten senses work on different frequencies and require a heck of a lot of work to get them to come even close to working together. Not everything works at the same pace either. Some parts of his body might be fast, some might be slow, and imagine having those two different processes in the same nervous system. Different frequencies and different intensities, how disorganizing is that?

So you have a child who's constantly going through his or her entire day trying to get just that right balance of feedback to feel organized. Needing different sensory input at different levels of intensity to be organized. How on earth are you going to get her sitting still, being quiet, not being allowed to move, and meet your needs when you have them? Being told that your needs must wait, you need to cope better, you need to hang on, wait until we're done with the lesson, wait for lunch.

Have you ever had an experience where something just wasn't going to wait? Imagine if what's not going to wait is the very input that makes or breaks your ability to hold it together. Meltdowns are often the sum total of accumulated disorganization that reaches its peak, all that nervous energy that's going out because there's not enough input to bring it in and organize it. The more time you spend disorganized and disregulated, the faster you escalate. Meltdowns are often called behavior. They're not. They're a state of extreme disregulation. Once an autistic child blows off that energy, then she can start calming down and, I hope, get her needs met again so she can feel organized.

My eldest boy is very much like me: highly auditory. If he could walk around listening to his Smartphone that plays movies and music all day long, he would. He needs to fall asleep listening to a movie in his ear because the sound regulates him. If you are disregulated, are you calm? Probably not.

Problems sleeping

Try and go to sleep at night when you're disregulated. The kids who won't stay in bed have to walk the halls and toss and turn; they not focused, they're not calm and they're not integrated. My middle son often needs my wife or I to squeeze his calves to calm him down. This gives him the proprioceptive input he needs to organize his nervous system so it can calm down. Ironically, I often need the same thing. My mind will be racing and I'll be unable to sleep, then my wife will squeeze my calf muscles for about ten minutes and I'll fall right to sleep. I know, what if there isn't anyone to squeeze your muscles to help you calm down?

Deep pressure is only one technique. The kind of calm, focused breathing learned through meditation is very helpful as well, as is stretching such as that taught in yoga.

Some kids like to have a story read to them because they get to listen to the soothing sounds of a parent's voice as they drift off to sleep. They're more auditory. Some kids need to snuggle, have a nice, tight hug. Some people like to fall asleep watching TV—more visual input organizes them.

When touch hurts

Now that we have discussed temperature and pressure, let's discuss pain. Some of the kids, like my youngest, slam their knees into the ground and don't seem to feel pain when they do it. In my son's case, his pain receptors are hyposensitive—underresponsive. He has bruises all up and down his legs. There are people who can cut themselves and not realize it until they notice blood.

Then there are the kids you barely touch but they react so strongly you'd think you'd cut their arm off because the touch hurts. I, for one, am highly sensitive to light touches. I like deep pressure as much as anybody else, but it has to be the right kind of pressure. If someone brushes my leg as they pass me, like in a movie theater going in and out of the seat, it can be so overwhelming that I have to fight the urge to push the person away from me. Therefore, I get there early so I can find that strategically placed seat where nobody will come across me in any way. If I sit in a seat where multiple people will brush against me, it can become so overwhelming that it is hard for me to breathe at times. I'll be so guarded that I'll hold my breath until the person passes. I start to feel panicky if three people come by me at once. So knowing that about myself, I need to put myself someplace where that won't happen.

Now for a child in a classroom, what options have they? Almost none. Then there's waiting in line. A child with hypersensitive skin has good reason to fear standing in line. Being brushed up against repeatedly threatens their organization, and their need to remain calm and focused.

Sometimes the fear of being touched is enough to escalate a child, especially if the child is already disregulated and is afraid one more sensory assault will push her over the edge. She may be thinking, "What if another person touches me? What if the person behind me, who I can't see, accidentally bumps into me?"

Now let's say I have a light touch sensitivity and vestibular issues, which I do. If I have vestibular balance issues, do I want to be moved? Of course not. If somebody bumps into me, I might move, and will have to regain my balance. So when the line starts to move, "Oh, my goodness, somebody's gonna touch me." So what's the solution? I want to be first or last in line whenever possible so I can create some distance between myself and the other people in line.

Others often mistake wanting to be in front of the line as strictly a desire by your child to be in control. Maybe that's part of it, but there's so much more to it. It is also that he wants to be in control of the aspects of the situation that most upset his nervous system. I am fortunate in that I have done the hard work of looking at myself at depths most people resist doing, and am confident enough in who I am to share these insights with you. But how would a child know these things about herself? How would an adult who doesn't know this information guide a child into understanding this about herself?

It may sound impossible but it isn't for those who are teachable and willing to learn. For those who aren't, your child is at the mercy of their assumptions about who she is and why she does what she does. The assumptions they make are typically judgmental and color the feedback they give a child who is simply trying to get her needs met.

How do you manage?

Here's a scenario in which we helped our five-year-old increase his awareness of his auditory sensitivity and the solution for managing it. He is very visual and enjoys going to the movie theater. But he needs earplugs and headphones to sit through the movie. How did we realize he needed this accommodation?

When we first started taking him to movies he refused to stay in his seat. He would climb over the chairs, annoy his brothers, walk up and down the aisle and ask to go to the bathroom every ten minutes. We'd end up missing the movie. One day he was walking past the television and a commercial came on that was loud and he quickly covered his ears. We hadn't seen him do that before. So we observed him and noticed him covering his ears a lot when watching the television. We asked him if certain sounds in particular were too loud and he was able to nod yes. The first thing we did was teach him to adjust the volume on the television.

My wife introduced him to the brand of foam earplugs she uses when things get too loud for her. It took some getting used to as you can imagine. When we tried them at the theater we realized they weren't enough and added headphones. Once we did that he was able to sit through the movie and enjoy it. More importantly, he now asks for them in other settings, such as restaurants when things become too loud for him.

This is the same child who likes to bang and crash to get proprioceptive input. Remember what I said earlier about a nervous system that has different parts working on different frequencies? Well, this son is hyposensitive when it comes to pain but hypersensitive when it comes to sound. So one part of his nervous system can barely handle input, while another needs tons of it. Teachers, please remember this point before saying, "Well, this student is so good in this subject, he should be able to do well in all the others." The same principle applies.

Since we know this about our son, we come prepared to the movie theater. We give him what he needs so he can sit there and be visually engaged. He loves music, but he loves it even more if there's a music video that goes along with it because he wants to watch it. For example, there was a song I played for him because I'm very auditory. I liked the way it sounded and wanted to see if he liked it. He responded, "No, I don't like that song." I got curious, went on the internet, and found the music video for that song. When I showed that to him, his face lit up and he said, "Oh, that's my favorite song." Now he can't get enough of it.

One thing I want to mention is that in terms of the foam earplugs, he wasn't comfortable with them at first. We kept reminding him what specific problem the earplugs could solve for him. So he was willing to wear them for a few minutes at a time until he got used to them. Now he requests them when things are too loud.

However, if your child is opposed to the earplugs, see if you can find some other sound that can be played in the background that is either closer to him or louder than, for example, the air conditioning, to cancel it out. Listening to music through an mp3 player works well for this.

But the potty scares me!

Here's an example of how, no matter how much you know about the spectrum or your own child, you can still miss something significant. Another challenge my five-year-old appeared to be having was bladder control issues. He wet his pants on almost a daily basis. I suspected that he lacked certain body awareness as part of being on the autism spectrum. He seeks nonstop proprioceptive input all day long just to feel coordinated (meaning he seeks high-impact play, somersaults and watches TV standing on his head).

Then one morning from his own mouth I learned that his pants wetting was due to an entirely different issue. He walked in on me that morning as I was using the bathroom and he asked why I was doing that. I told him I use the potty because I had to go and didn't want to have an accident. I suggested that was why he needed to use the potty He responded, "But the potty scares me." When I was done I sat down with him to learn more about what he meant.

We were already aware that he had a significant hearing sensitivity and didn't want to flush the toilet after going to the bathroom because the sound of the flush hurt his ears. What we didn't realize was that it hurt so much that he'd rather wet himself than have to endure either the sound of the flushing or my wife or I asking him to go back and flush the toilet, thus subjecting himself to the pain.

I encouraged him to share this revelation with my wife Cathy, who in her infinite creativity and wisdom proposed the following remedy. He would go potty instead of having accidents by covering his right ear with his right hand, placing his left ear on his shoulder, and using his left hand to flush the toilet.

We tried it and he gave a big smile after his first success. In reviewing it he said the sound still hurt though not as much. The ultimate solution ended up being an inexpensive pair of earmuffs. When wearing them he said the sound no longer hurt his ears.

Now I hope I don't confuse you too much with this next one, but keep in mind that the human nervous system is a complex place to live. So if certain sounds are annoying and disregulate a person, other sounds will regulate. I've had parents ask me why their teenager will listen to music full blast with no problem but become very angry at the sound of someone chewing food. It's because a single sense can be disregulated to the point where certain sounds calm while others escalate. For me, mid-tones are just right while high pitches or low pitches cause me pain.

Emotions running high

Now what I'm about to explain is extremely important so please listen closely. There are stereotypes about spectrumites lacking empathy and sometimes lacking emotion. This couldn't be further from the truth. What spectrumites often have tremendous difficulty with is managing and regulating the intensity of emotions. As such, we often need to discover strategies to assist with regulating our emotions. I find that music is a powerful tool for helping me regulate my mood. If I'm anxious, there are certain songs that will calm me. If I'm tired, certain songs will wake me up. If I'm afraid, there are songs that will help me relax and engage in a situation.

Looking at a sunset, a certain picture, a certain color, or the act of drawing or doodling, calms some people who are far more visual. For kinesthetics, perhaps a fidget or manipulating things with their hands is calming. Even certain kinds of stretches or physical movements can be very regulating. I've discovered ways to subtly and strategically give myself proprioceptive input in social situations that helps me regulate, but no one around me even notices that I'm doing anything special.

Here's a primary example. I used to have a job that would require weekly meetings lasting a few hours. The meetings were in a cramped conference room with poor ventilation and hard plastic chairs. So we were close together, which assaulted my touch sensitivity by the mere possibility of being touched. The poor ventilation affected my temperature sensitivity as the temperature in the room rose with all the people in there. The hard chairs hit certain pressure points in my behind and legs, which triggered my hypersensitive pain receptors. Imagine a child in a classroom with these issues who is expected to sit for hours with all of this going on and is discouraged from regulating him or herself.

I would get so disregulated in these meetings I'd become angry. So now I had to regulate my senses and my mood. A few things I'd do included using the heels of my hands to press firmly on the tendon just above my kneecaps or the middle of my thigh muscles. This would relax me quickly. I could also rub the muscle at the base of one thumb with the other thumb, and I frequently do this in all situations. Now the best strategy I have found for myself in these situations is to rest the ankle of one leg on the knee of the other in a figure four position. Then I slowly apply pressure to the inside of the knee of the leg that is crossed. As I do this, I feel a slow, steady stretch in my hip joint, and when I reach the ideal point in the stretch, I feel my whole body relax. It's wonderful when I'm able to do this. Experiment with this stretch and see if it works for you. You can even switch legs and stretch both hips. For people who have extremely flexible joints, however, their joints may be too loose to feel a stretch so this technique wouldn't benefit them and they can find another way. But I hope this will be helpful for many of you.

When your emotions are more than you can handle

Now let me explain more about emotional intensity. When you think of the intensity of light, sound, or touch being overwhelming and difficult to manage, the intensity of emotion is often more difficult to manage. The reason is because light, sound, or touch come from one direction, outside in. There are things we can do to block it out.

When it comes to emotion, emotion expressed by others triggers emotions in us. So now we need to regulate the emotions coming from the other person as well as the emotions stirring in ourselves. If emotions such as fear or anger come at us fast and with a high level of intensity, it happens faster than we can regulate it. That's why you see such extreme displays of emotion from many of us. It's like a pipe bursting and then we scramble to contain it or get the energy out until we begin to calm on our own.

Some spectrumites I work with have come to realize that they avoid showing emotion and being around others, who are intense personalities or highly emotional because emotions, are particularly difficult for them to regulate. They're called cold, distant, and lacking empathy by others, when in truth they fear the disregulating power of emotions, so they avoid it.

Recently I was speaking to a group of parents who had a common experience in that whenever one of them became upset, their spectrum child would quickly run up to them and say, "I'm sorry," even if he didn't do anything. I explained the following to them, which might help you, too. Their children do this in the hope that an apology will prevent you from becoming angry. Anger is the hardest emotion for us to regulate, and when we see it coming, we want to stop it, and many kids have learned that you apologize to make a person feel better. Does this make sense?

A teacher shared with me that she had a student on the spectrum who tried to run from the classroom every time she raised her voice in order to get the attention of her students. This is, of course, because the intensity of her voice came out of nowhere and with more intensity than he could handle, so he tried to get away from it to prevent being overloaded by it. He was probably not consciously aware of any more than wanting to get away from something that upset him.

So how do you support a child who has this sensitivity? As luck would have it, we had a similar situation with my middle son. His second-grade teacher yelled a lot, and although he wouldn't run, he'd basically shut down because he never knew when she'd yell again. The mistake she made was when she saw him get upset, she'd go over to him and say she wasn't yelling at him and wasn't it unfortunate that the behavior of other students required her to yell.

What she missed is this: Even though she wasn't yelling at him, he was in the presence of her emotional intensity. Though the effect it had on the other students was to get their attention, for him it rattled him to the point where it was difficult for him to get organized again.

So here was the solution I proposed and it worked beautifully. When she knew she was going to yell, she'd walk over to him and place her hand on his shoulder, which cued him that it was coming. He'd then cover his ears, and when she was done, he'd uncover his ears. This completely removed the surprise element of the yelling as well as allowing him to buffer the intensity. It's wonderful when the solutions are so simple.

Chapter 6

Coming to Your Senses

It's one thing when you have ten senses that don't work together in a coordinated fashion, now let's discuss an interesting sensory challenge that occurs around the experience of auditory processing. Keep in mind, I'm no expert on the neurological aspects of auditory processing challenges, but I can tell you what it feels like when it's happening. Imagine that your ear can hear just fine but when the signals from the ear reach the brain, the brain doesn't effectively organize the information the ear is sending it.

The school systems provide basic hearing tests to kids that determine if the child can hear certain tones. That doesn't tell them anything about a child's ability to process complex sounds like human speech, especially in a classroom with so many different sounds to be processed at once.

My sons all passed their school-administered hearing tests, only to have comprehension difficulties when being spoken to. In my case, there are times, especially when I'm disregulated, when I'm tired, I'm not able to focus as well, when somebody will be talking to me, and all of a sudden their mouth is moving and nothing's coming out. It's like my brain has decided not to hear anymore. At some point my ears just stop hearing. There are other times when a person's voice sounds like it's cutting out—I'll catch every other word. It sounds like their voice is shaky and wavy, going in, going out—sometimes it's like that.

So one of the ways I compensate for this, whenever I can, is to have conversations in very quiet areas. That's the best way for me to hear everything coming out of a person's mouth. But if you're in a classroom and you have auditory processing issues, it's hard enough to hear the voice of the teacher; now you have a kid messing with papers next to you, you have sounds out in the hall, you have the kids laughing or making noise in the next classroom. It can be nearly impossible to make sense of all that input.

The auditory smoothy

What happens at this point in a spectrumite's brain goes beyond simply being distracted. Too many sustained noises at one time overload his brain's ability to sort them out and they all kind of run together into one big noise. It's like an auditory smoothy. You put all the different sounds into a blender and grind them all together until you can't tell them apart anymore. Then he gets criticized for being off task, not focusing, not paying attention to the teacher like he's supposed to. Good luck. It's not going to work when your brain doesn't know how to sort things out, how to prioritize or discriminate between what you want to pay attention to and what you are supposed to ignore.

Does the spectrum brain multitask or does it unitask? It unitasks; it works best on one thing at a time. So in other words, all you do is hear. You don't hear this and not hear that. You hear everything. You just hear. So if there are a lot of sounds around you, you hear it all. You're in a movie theater with all kinds of sounds, you're in a classroom with all kinds of sounds, and you're in a mall or restaurant with all kinds of sounds. You hear everything. So if you ever catch yourself saying to your child, "Just ignore it" or, "You need to learn to cope better," I hope you now realize what an unsympathetic and absurd request you're making. Their brains simply don't do what you're asking. Their brains won't rewire themselves on the spot to accommodate the needs of the parent, the teacher, or the classroom. You must meet the child halfway. That's what we did with my youngest, as I mentioned earlier, so he can enjoy being in a movie theater for the entire movie.

When working to find the halfway point with each person, there are no "one size fits all" strategies to regulate a spectrumite's nervous system. I hear a common cliché in the spectrum world that if you meet one spectrum child, you've met one spectrum child. It's used more philosophically than in actual practice because I encounter far too many people approaching a child from a "one size fits all" approach. The other approach I see is to randomly apply interventions at the child to see what sticks, instead of taking the time to get to know the child and then custom fitting the intervention to the child.

Stop sweating

It's also important to remember that a child's difficulty handling an overwhelming environment isn't a matter of motivation or endurance. Telling them to try harder is absurd. Let's take a moment and think about something your body does automatically that you cannot control. Any thoughts? Things like blinking, breathing, your heartbeat. Let's use sweating for this example. If someone is sweating a lot, does it make sense to tell him to stop it? Would you say, "Come on, cool down. You know, put your mind to it. You're not trying hard enough." It doesn't make sense, does it?

But that's what you're asking of these kids. Their nervous system doesn't just do that. There's no technique to do it, unless it's a technique that gives specific feedback to the unique needs of that child's nervous system. So if a child needs to sit still and she's very kinesthetic, you have things like weighted vests. What's the problem with those things? They may fall off. The benefit is temporary if at all. In addition, the basic premise of a weighted vest is a problem. The premise is that any pressure will do. If you need deep pressure, maybe you need it on one spot on your body. The best place to give me deep pressure is on my shoulders, calves, and thighs. The more stressed I am, the bigger the muscle you need to press on so I get more proprioception more quickly. Weighted vests don't automatically get heavier as a child gets more stressed. So if I'm overloaded, putting a little weight on my shoulders for a long period of time would probably do more to make my neck sore than it would to decrease my tension. So what options do we have then?

Sit up straight and don't pay attention

You need to start by questioning everything you assume to be true about how a child functions best in the classroom. The idea that "eyes front, sitting up straight" equals paying attention is a lie when it comes to spectrumites. You need to learn what each child needs in order to pay attention, and each child needs to get to know himself or herself.

I had a client with such low muscle tone that he had to rest his body and head on his desk the entire class. The teacher was incredibly mean to him and accused him of being disrespectful, lazy, not getting enough sleep, and of not paying attention. Who do you think actually had the problem in this situation? The teacher.

This was a teacher with a very narrow definition of what it means to pay attention. I made the revolutionary suggestion (sarcasm) that the teacher ask him a question from time to time to see if he was paying attention. What do you suspect she discovered? That he was listening. You see, if he had committed all of his energy to sitting up straight, eyes front, he would have had very little left to actually pay attention. So in taking care of himself by laying his head on the desk, he was able to pay attention. Unfortunately the teacher in this case was unteachable. Although she learned he was paying attention, her limited thinking required him to pay attention her way and she ended up taking his desk away.

In response to that his parents demanded he be removed from that class and placed with another teacher or they wouldn't return him to school. Their response was that there were no other classes he could attend, so they gave him a study hall instead. This is a case of an inflexible system failing a child with unique needs. And the inflexibility lay more in their thinking than in their actual options.

A colleague shared with me the case of a young man who insisted on reading the newspaper throughout class, and it upset the teachers, who considered it disruptive. I asked if he was noisy when he did it. They said no, but it was disruptive simply because he was doing it. But other than appearances, what problems did it cause? The social worker working with this young man said that it was inappropriate. Here again is a case of extremely limited thinking, because it stepped outside their narrow definition of how students are permitted to pay attention. It turned out that the young man was, in fact, paying attention and could answer virtually any question asked of him. Reading the newspaper helped him focus, and to take it from him made him agitated and unable to focus. The newspaper was an accommodation unique to him as opposed to the stereotypical weighted vest or some other strategy in the "one size fits all" toolbox of the public school system.

In unique situations like the ones I just mentioned, I consistently hear school staff refer to the spectrum child as manipulative. For the record, in my experience, when an adult accuses a child of being manipulative, it's because the adult resents a child for not doing something the adult's way and the adult would rather have the child submit than meet the child halfway. The greatest successes I have seen have always been when the teacher and the student both had their needs respected and accommodated in order for learning to take place. The result was a student who felt respected, gaining in confidence and trust in the teacher, and a teacher who grew as a person and as an educator. That is a beautiful example of a win–win outcome.

I need a dinosaur hug

An important question arises at this point, how do you meet a child halfway when he hasn't developed his self-awareness and you don't know how to help him develop it? I'll use an example of something we did with my five-year-old. We sure do talk about him a lot, don't we? Not to worry, the other two will have their turn. Please pay very close attention to the wording in this example because the wording is everything. We're talking now about increasing a spectrum child's awareness of what his sensory needs are in terms of how to self-regulate.

Now let me remind you that our five-year-old is a banger and a crasher and needs a lot of proprioceptive input to regulate his nervous system. One of the best ways for him to get this is through hugging, but like a weighted vest, any old hug won't do. Through talking with him in a very strategic way, we've established five different types of hugs depending on what his sensory needs are, and he tells us which one he needs. Now let's discuss how we helped him get there.

He used to get his hugs ambush style. He'd just run up to me or anyone else and hug their leg as hard as he could. Sometimes he'd knock the person off balance, and get scolded for it. I used to scold him for this, too. Sometimes he'd come up behind me and grab me around the waist and scare the heck out of me.

One day I asked him why he kept doing that. With a little pouty lip, he said, "I want a hug." So I knelt on one leg and gave him a hug and he hugged me tightly. I asked him if he felt better and he said, "Yes," and ran off to play. Knowing what I know about the spectrum, I realized he needed deep pressure, knew how to get it, but, being five and being on the spectrum, he didn't know how to effectively get what he needed so he just did it. So I began working with him to teach him the language and reciprocity behind getting a hug when he needs it. I teach parents how to have this conversation with their children to achieve the same outcome. Are you ready to learn this?

First, you need to have your mind-set in place. When your child or student does something outside of the norm for you, it is critical that you see it as something designed to meet a need The moment you judge it as inappropriate, you've blown it. Because that judgment makes you want to change it, when what you need to do is understand it. Are you with me on this (because this is crucial)?

Why that?

Your first responsibility is to be teachable and seek to understand the need your child or student is trying to meet. The first question you must ask yourself when you experience a spectrum child doing something unique is, "Why that?" Of all the things the child could be doing right now, "Why that?" "What problem is this child trying to solve for himself?" *No*, it isn't simply to get attention, that's a lazy rationalization given by people who don't want to do the work to examine it more closely.

"Why that?" is how Cathy and I began the exploration of helping our son discover his five types of hugs. The outcomes we achieved were that he was able to communicate the hug he needed and demonstrate it, as well as experiencing how these skills will generalize, and generalization is the truest measure of the value of any skill.

An important point I need to acknowledge is that whereas our son was a willing participant, many parents experience children who won't ask or even say, "I don't need a break, I don't need help," when they clearly do. They refuse help from their parents and the professionals in their lives.

To begin changing this resistance, start by examining the relationship between her and the person she's resisting help from. What role does she see the person playing in her life? Many spectrumites get sick of the therapies and everyone wanting to help all the time because it sends the message that they're helpless. They also aren't given the option by their parents or teachers to say no. They're made to be helped and at some point will exercise the right to set boundaries and say, "I don't need it, I don't want it, leave me alone."

So how then do you support your children in getting the help they need? You begin with the question, "Why that?" and then partner with your child in a way that makes him an active part of the process of being helped instead of simply a recipient of it. In the absence of this, a child may interpret the role of any professional as: "I'm the expert. I'm in charge, and you do what I tell you, I'm setting the agenda, we're not discussing it, we're here to do this, I have this clipboard with this list of goals that we haven't negotiated, or discussed what you need to achieve, and this is what you're going to do, and I'm going to check you off if you're noncompliant." Now I've met many OTs and other professionals who work to establish a relationship with a child first, and with my coaching, they learn to partner and become even more effective. Does that make sense?

Now let's discuss how we partnered with our five-year-old Connor to establish his five different kinds of hugs. Cathy initiated it with this routine when he got home from preschool. He'd get off the school bus and she'd be waiting for him at the door. The moment he reached her he'd break down and begin crying because he was so overloaded from school. So she would sit on the floor next to him and say, "OK, you seem like you're not very happy. Can you tell me what's wrong?" He'd say, "I don't know." She'd ask, "OK, are you hurt?" "No." "Do you think you're sad?" "Yes." "OK, do you know why you're sad?" "No." "Well, is there something that I could do that might make you feel better?" "Yes."

"OK, can you tell me?" "I need a hug." So Cathy would hug him and then ask, "Does that work?" "No, I'm still sad." "OK, do we need to do something different?" "Yes." "What do you think you need?" "Tighter." So over time by asking him specifically how he needed the hug, adjusted according to how he was feeling, we developed a hug system so he now has the right hug for the job depending on how he's feeling.

Now when he comes home he'll say he wants a Connor hug, which means he's had a good day and he just wants a general hug to give him some quick pressure to calm down a little, a few pats on the back, and he's off and running. We also have the bear hug, which is a tighter and slightly longer Connor hug. He'll say, "I'm done," when he's had enough.

The dinosaur hug is a very deep pressure hug, but he wants you to growl in his ear while you're doing it. This adds a little auditory input as well to help regulate him. Then we've got the fish hug or a fishy hug, where he wants you to pick him up, hold him very tightly, and wiggle him so that his legs swing and he gets to dangle and feel a stretch as well. Of course as he gets bigger we'll have to renegotiate that one to avoid injury.

One of the keys to this process is asking your child, "Can you either tell me or show me what you need me to do?" A nonverbal child may need to show you. However, many children won't have any awareness of their needs under these circumstances. So what do you do then? You offer a hug and then ask for feedback while hugging him, "Do you need it tighter?" He may honestly respond, "I don't know." In that case, you ask if you can make it tighter to see if it helps. When he gives you the permission to do so, you do it, hold it a few seconds, and ask, "Does this feel better?" If the child says yes, you're good to go. You're using both language and action when helping your child discover the strategy. Do you want it tighter, do you want it looser? You're saying it as you're doing it so he associates the feeling with the language. Then you encourage him to use the same language when requesting it. In terms of something like a fishy hug, you can negotiate that to be given by certain people. But a bear hug can be easily described and asked for from others.

The fifth kind of hug Connor enjoys is when you hold him while he sits on your lap and you both rock back and forth. It's extremely calming and comforting for him. It gives him proprioceptive and vestibular input when he's had a hard day. This may sound like a lot to go through, especially for adults who reserve the right to guess and assume when it comes to their children or students. The approach I've just explained begins from the belief that your child knows the answer but you must work together to find it. It can be difficult to embrace an approach like this that seems counterintuitive. In time it can become second nature.

The eleventh sense

I know I said earlier that we have ten senses. But I'd like to introduce you to an interesting sensory experience that many people are unfamiliar with. It's one that could be considered an eleventh sense. It's called synesthesia. Are you familiar with that word? *Synesthesia* occurs when an experience through one sense triggers a simultaneous experience in a different sense. For example, there are those who see colors when they hear music. My wife and brother-in-law have this experience.

Again, I'm not an expert on it and my research hasn't come up with a test for it either. But I can share with you the experience of it. The way an experience of synesthesia is typically described is in terms of the sense that is initially stimulated and then the second sense that is triggered. So when I experience auditory-vestibular synesthesia, it refers to the experience of hearing very low vibrations that give me a sense of movement that makes me sick to my stomach.

Another form of synesthesia I experience is when the sound of a person's voice causes a sense of pressure in different parts of my body. It's interesting that I feel the voice of each member of my family in a different place. I don't discuss this much because I don't want people asking me where I feel their voice. But in the case of my family, I feel my wife's voice in my chest, upper arms, and the sides of my head. When my eldest son talks to me, I feel it in the sides of my head. When my middle son talks to me, I feel it in my throat, chest, and stomach. When my youngest son talks to me, I feel it in my eyes, forehead, the sides of my head, and chest.

An important point to make here is that the sensations aren't pleasant or unpleasant; they just feel like light pressure in those areas. However, if a person's voice is too deep or is yelling, I feel the pressure in my solar plexus and it's hard to breathe. But overall it's quite an interesting experience and adds another layer to the experience of listening to people talk.

As if this auditory experience of the world weren't complex enough, let's add another layer with auditory-visual synesthesia. This results in my seeing the words that are being spoken to me. When I'm listening to a friend or client speak, I can see each word they say scroll through the air. This way I'm reading it as well as hearing it. This allows me to catch every word a person says. If a word repeats itself in a conversation, sometimes I see it in darker color (like bold type); if a person emphasizes that word while speaking, it literally jumps out at me like 3D.

Now this can get overwhelming in a room full of people because I begin not only hearing and feeling their voices, but seeing their words as well. It can saturate me quickly, so crowded places without earplugs or my mp3 player to drown it out cause big problems for me.

In my consulting work, I've helped clients identify sensory experiences they didn't realize they were having. Experiences that others would dismiss as impatience or "being too emotionally sensitive." Though these are legitimate issues, it's difficult to get support from others when neither they nor the spectrumite even know what's going on. Once we identified the issue and developed strategies to manage it, things changed for the better.

This is why it is so important to realize that there are many ways to experience the sensory information in the world around us. When something doesn't bother you but someone else responds as though she's in pain, don't respond by telling her it's no big deal and to stop being such a wimp. It's ignorant and cruel to minimize someone else's experience like that. A more enlightened parent, educator or friend would support her by validating her experience.

Supersensitivity

Here are a few more points about sensory experiences that might never occur to you. As I mentioned, if a sound is too low, it can be hard for me to breathe. It's important to note that the longer the sound lasts, the worse the experience gets. For example, there was one time several years ago when I was sitting in a restaurant, and one of the busboys rolled a big rumbling cart down the aisle, right past me. The closer it got, the more intense the vibration was, and of course the more intense the pressure on my solar plexus became. I kept hoping he'd get past me before I had a panic attack. Now, who on earth would know this would be such a problem for me? Most people may simply notice this rumbling cart, then tune it out and go back to whatever they were doing. For me it was a nearly paralyzing sensory experience.

Then there was the time I went to the dentist to get my teeth cleaned and the hygienist used a new tool with an incredibly high-pitched motor. The moment she turned it on I felt a sharp searing pain in my ears so intense I froze and couldn't speak until she turned it off. This is an example of a sensory experience that I call a supersensitivity. The solution in my case is to listen to music while I get my teeth cleaned. Now if the dentist needs to use a drill I require heavy sedation because my pain receptors are so supersensitive that even with seven or more shots of novocaine, I still feel everything the dentist is doing. It's just one of the many quirks of being me.

It is frustrating sometimes to have so many things to accommodate, but you know what? That's my reality. It's also true that every one of my problems has a solution, and I've become one dynamite problem solver, as you can see. I simply refuse to define my life by my problems. I define it instead by solving those problems and teaching those solutions to others.

Being choosy

I've been asked how on earth I get through the day with all these challenges. Very strategically, that's how. I choose where I go, when I go, and who I spend time with, options denied to young spectrumites on a daily basis, unfortunately.

I wasn't even aware of my sensory issues until adulthood after learning I was on the spectrum. Consulting with an OT and talking with others on the spectrum helped me put language to a lot of these experiences that I couldn't understand myself, let alone explain to others.

Throughout my life I mostly remember being overwhelmed whenever anybody would talk to me. Now for many spectrumites who shut down when you talk to them, some of it might be the social anxiety that stems from having no idea what to do in that situation. But there might be other layers to it. We simply don't know unless we help our kids get to know themselves, in large part by being their student, walking the journey of self-discovery with them, so they can learn to define their unique experience of the world and then explain it to us as best they can. Think of it as an experience of coming into their senses, becoming fully aware of their experience. Once they're aware, they can be choosier about what they expose themselves to in order to find the right balance for themselves.

Finding balance

With so much sensory disregulation it's a real struggle to find balance. Every day of my life is an ongoing concentrated effort to stay regulated, calm and focused. Ultimately what's required is to keep my life very simple, very meticulous and very predictable. Why? Because if I know exactly what I'm going to be exposed to through the course of a day (as much as possible), I can plan to avoid things that will disregulate me and surround myself with things that will help me stay calm and focused.

Yes, spectrumites like order and predictability, but it's not because we're controlling, it's because we're protecting ourselves from disregulation. We don't want be pulled in ten different directions because we have ten different sensory pathways, and at any given time some are up, some are down, and they're always in competition with each other. We just want to surround ourselves and create a world for ourselves that allows us to maintain some sense of stability. That's why we construct the lives around us that we do.

I may be able to stand in front of a large audience and speak very articulately because verbal ability happens to be my forte and something I've spent years refining. However, I have the math skills of a fifth grader, need to count on my fingers, am incapable of remembering anything unless I write it down, and without my ADD meds I'd be scattered and restless with difficulty starting, let alone finishing, a task. I have significant dysgraphia, making it difficult to sign my own name without concentrating—thank goodness I can type everything else. With all these challenges, many of them shared with my own children and many of my clients, it is crucial to understand the following point. All of the social stories and medications in the world will not help you if what you need is sensory input.

Well, how do you even know what input you need? As a parent you can watch your child and see what type of sensory input he seeks and what kind he avoids. I also highly recommend having an occupational therapist who specializes in sensory integration evaluate your child.

Another way you can tell is by looking at what your child's special interests are. Look at how she spends the majority of her time. How does she calm down? What are the activities she chooses to the exclusion of all others? Take the child who wants to sit quietly by herself and read all day long—is this a child looking for a tremendous amount of auditory input? Is this a child looking for a lot of kinesthetic input? This is a child engaging the world through her eyes. I do much better with an audio book than I ever do with a written one. When I try to read, it's frustrating and exhausting. My eyes don't track well so I'm always losing my place. I might get through a page or two and have to read the same paragraph several times before I comprehend anything. I listen to an audio book and absorb the information like a sponge.

My eldest son needs to listen to things all the time. My youngest needs to watch things. My middle boy, who has incredible academic challenges, which are taught primarily through visual and auditory means, is very kinesthetic. For the longest time we didn't know what he was good at. Then one day he asked, "Can I learn to crack an egg? Can I help in the kitchen?" Last year for Christmas we got him a chef's hat, and he wears it every time he helps with the cooking. He wants to be the one to flip the burgers. He wants to scramble the eggs. He wants to help. He wants to move. He wants to step up on the stool and reach for things from a shelf. He may decide to be a chef because he loves to interact with the kitchen environment through his body and feels competent there. He even volunteers to empty the dishwasher and shovel snow. And no, you can't borrow him.

He has taught me so much about how limiting a classroom can be, and how liberating it can be to be educated outside the classroom in a world where he can engage it according to his strengths instead of according to what's appropriate. Like many spectrumites, his gifts are contextual. He may never get straight As, he may never be valedictorian, but he'll probably learn to cook you the best meal you've ever eaten and get paid handsomely for it.

He found what he's good at and wants to do it as often as possible because doing so gives him the experience of feeling effective and competent, and teaches him that he has something to offer the world. In the classroom he hears, "Try harder. You can do better." What the teacher thinks is motivating is actually criticism. Yes, he did well, but it's not good enough. Try harder. You can do more. In the kitchen, where it's very concrete—the dishwasher was full, now it is empty—it's very measurable. He finds a better balance between his needs and abilities when he's allowed to experiment with different contexts. The school system doesn't have that kind of flexibility, but life does.

It's important to realize that teachers are typically very limited in what they're allowed to do in their own classrooms. The curriculum is standardized instead of individualized and doesn't lend itself easily to individual learning styles. I've met some magnificent teachers who aren't allowed to be as creative as they'd like to be and are actually held back as much as their students. Another challenge teachers face is when their own learning style differs greatly from their students. If a teacher is highly visual herself, it can be very difficult to teach a kinesthetic child because the teacher would have to work extra-hard, perhaps at her own expense. Matching teaching style with learning style whenever possible is important.

The problem with research

Now I want to share something that may sound controversial, but it's a huge pet peeve of mine. I get frustrated when I hear the words "research-based" used as though it's the holy grail of credibility for working with spectrum kids. What it is is a double-edged sword. On the one hand, it can be helpful in determining strategies that can generalize to many kids on the spectrum. On the other hand, damage is done when people use research to inform what they do and forget that the most important research you need to do is to get to know the child you're working with and do what's right for her. Anyone who claims to use a protocol without any modification is either lying or unaware of the adjustments they're making. You must ultimately custom fit general research-based ideas and strategies to the person you are working with.

I'm no scientist; I'm not an academic whiz, and when I read scientific literature, it might as well be written in ancient Egyptian. I rely heavily on empirical data. I'm not suggesting in any way that research be abandoned and replaced with reckless hit-or-miss approaches with a student until you find something that works—that would be irresponsible and unethical. I'm talking about using it as a basis for exploring what is ultimately true for each particular child. It's difficult to stereotype when you approach working with an individual this way. You will eventually find what is true for him by partnering with him and learning what works for him, taking the risks together and celebrating the successes together. That's how you find the data you need. That's the best and most reliable research. I do it with my own children and with my clients, and we all experience results that blow people's minds. It's all because of the work we do together. Life isn't lived in a lab or in a questionnaire. It's lived in our moments together, and that's where we find our successes; that's where we build the foundation for our sense of who we are and the value we have for other people. That's where we build the present that puts us on the path to creating the brighter future we were born to live.

Part 2 Creating Relationships that Work for Both of Us

Chapter 7

How to Build Self-Confidence in One Step

How confident are you? It's well known that confidence is something spectrumites struggle with, including me. We are going to discuss what confidence is, where you get it, how you lose it, and the one step you can take to build it and keep it. Are you ready?

What is confidence?

Let's define confidence so that we're thinking of and discussing it in the same way. We need to be on the same page if we're going to have understanding. How do you define *confidence*? When I've posed this question to others I've heard responses such as: confidence is having faith in your own abilities to act with effectiveness and feel like you are being able to succeed in life. Another put it simply as believing in yourself.

The common theme I hear in definitions of confidence is the importance of belief. With that, I'll offer my definition of *confidence*. *Confidence* is the belief in your ability to create meaningful results based on the experience of having done so. I'll break this definition down to help you understand why it is the one I use.

"The belief in the ability to create meaningful results"—I didn't say positive results; I said meaningful. *Meaningful* refers to the personal value a person places on the results. If you learn something from the results you create, they are meaningful and have value. You can learn a lot from experience, whether it went the way you wanted it to or not. It does not necessarily have to be positive. One of the more popular sayings is, "It is not what happens to you, it is what you do with what happens to you." I know many people use that advice to cheer each other up, but too few practice it. It is important that you understand the meaningfulness of it. What meaning you can extract from whatever experience you have? What are your thoughts on this?

Imposing your own limits

Some people to whom I've offered this definition of confidence state that confidence is also the result of the support we get from others, as well as the security that comes from making the right choices. That's a problematic way of viewing confidence as far as I'm concerned. Making the right choices as determined by whose standards? Other people's? Ultimately you need to benefit from whatever happens beyond whether others approve. Otherwise the only thing you accomplish is being a people pleaser.

If you follow the premise that confidence results from making the right decision, what happens when you don't get the results you want? What does that tell you about the steps you took and the decisions you made: that they weren't right either? If you are a spectrumite who tends toward all-or-nothing thinking, if the decision leads to the wrong outcome, then all of your thinking leading up to it is wrong. I've encountered spectrumites who are afraid to make decisions unless they're guaranteed to be correct. Imagine how completely paralyzing that belief is. Since as human beings, we frequently learn by the very fact that our decisions don't always lead to the right outcome, then how can someone who insists on a guaranteed right outcome before taking action ever learn anything? They can't. So how do we change that?

First, understand this: If the words you use are limiting, they are a reflection of the thoughts that created them, which are also limiting. For example, the use of the words *right* or *wrong* to describe the value of decisions. Is it really that clear-cut? Here's an exchange I had with a mother we'll call Mary to explore this point further. I asked her if decisions could be clearly defined as *right* or *wrong*.

MARY: Sometimes.

BRIAN: Can you offer me an example?

MARY: Sure. It's wrong to hit your little brother.

BRIAN: Why is it wrong?

MARY: Because it's mean.

BRIAN: Anything else?

MARY: It hurts his feelings.

BRIAN: What else?

MARY: Well, you're supposed to be nice to your siblings.

BRIAN: What else are you supposed to do?

MARY: Treat each other with respect and support one another.

BRIAN: And how do you teach these rules to your spectrum child?

MARY: Well, I know I'm not perfect, but I yell sometimes and take things away as punishment.

BRIAN: Thank you very much for being so courageous and so honest in sharing that. Let me tell you what I heard just now. What I heard wasn't that it's wrong to hit your little brother. What I heard is that it's important to treat your brother with respect and support. But what I hear you emphasizing with your child is what he's doing wrong, with little or no discussion about what to do instead—is that accurate?

MARY: Well, I do tell him to be nice to his brother.

BRIAN: Do you recall where that direction comes in when you're correcting him?

MARY: Well, I tell him to stop hitting his brother, and I think I say, "Be nice," but I'm not sure.

BRIAN: Is it safe to say the emphasis is on what he's doing that you don't like?

MARY: I suppose.

Message received

The exchange between Mary and me demonstrates a very important distinction. I'll explain this point now and it will become clearer as we go along. First, let's review the definition of *confidence* again. *Confidence* is the belief in your ability to create meaningful results based on the experience of having done so, right? So if the feedback our kids get from us is, "Stop hitting your brother, you're not being nice, you're being rude," what's the message we're sending in terms of the results he's getting? The message is that he's not nice and that he's rude. The more he receives this message the more he develops the belief that the results he's able to create are of not being nice and being rude.

You see it doesn't matter that you want him to be nice and be respectful, because you don't offer any guidance on how to do it. You put all of your energy into scolding and punishing when he isn't doing it. That's why you're getting the opposite of what you want. You're reinforcing what you don't want, and the result is that you get more of it. His confidence is based on his experience of the results he gets. The feedback you provide is a powerful component of that experience.

Now back to the original point of using words like *right* and *wrong*—with feedback like this, your child learns that he tends to make the wrong decisions. So the work to be done here is both on the feedback you give your child and the options your child believes he has when it comes to making a meaningful decision. As I mentioned, this will all become clearer as we move along in our discussion.

What's your experience?

Using our definition of confidence, your belief in your ability to create meaningful results is based on the experience of having done so. So, this goes beyond just believing it, believing you can, being positive, and thinking it is all going to work out— the experience of having been successful is critical. I work with spectrumites from young children to teens and adults as well as their parents and teachers. I can't begin to tell you how many parents say, "But I compliment my child all the time. I tell her how well she's doing. I say 'Great job' when she does something well and yet she still has low self-confidence." Many teachers I've worked with have made similar statements.

My clients (those on the spectrum) often say they try to think positive and are tired of being so negative but just can't seem to manage thinking positive. So, based upon the definition I have given you, what do you think is likely to be missing? I'll tell you what's missing. You can say to somebody until you are blue in the face that you believe in her, you think she can do anything and you think she's doing a great job. But if, in her mind, her experience contradicts you, then she will not agree with you. If in her mind, she has not had the experience of creating meaningful results, as far as she's concerned your compliment is a lie because she has no experience to back it up.

So in order to think positively about yourself, to believe in yourself, the belief needs to be based on experience. She must have had the experience of being competent because competence is the root of confidence. Competent means you are effective at creating results. If she does not have the experience of competence, she will not have confidence. The experience comes from doing it, seeing it, and feeling that result. Does that make sense?

I'm not content to believe in myself simply because someone believes in me. I'm not saying that it doesn't help; it is necessary to have the support of others. But if I have not experienced firsthand doing something that I cared about, when I felt effective, and was able to say, "Look at what I did!" in celebration of my results, my experience will always trump taking another person's word for it.

It's important to note that you can feel competent in some areas of your life and not others. I spoke to the mother of a young spectrumite recently who shared that she feels competent at work because she's held the job for eight years and is very respected by her colleagues. Yet when it comes to taking care of herself she feels incompetent. She's created a life centered on taking care of everyone else, especially her daughter on the spectrum. Then when she does feel like taking care of herself she feels bad about it because the feedback she gets in life reinforces feeling competent when she's taking care of others and not when she's taking care of herself. She clearly had significant imbalance in her feelings of confidence.

The problem with compliments

I asked her if anyone had complimented her on things in which she lacked confidence. She had, as many of us have experienced.

Her response to these compliments (that she did not agree with) was the obligatory, "Thank you." She shared that although her response isn't heartfelt and while the compliment actually made her uncomfortable, the person complimenting her was being nice so she wanted to be polite. The point is that her experience in that area is that she lacks competence, so a compliment from someone else isn't enough to change her mind.

Have you ever said, "Thank you," in response to a compliment for which you felt unworthy? Have you ever responded more honestly and yet politely? Let me give you an example. Someone has complimented you on a job well done in an area where you do not feel competent and you downplay it. You say it is no big deal or you could have done better or anybody else could have done it. Have you ever responded in that way either out loud or in your own mind? I know I have.

Have you ever faked gratitude with a statement such as an enthusiastic, "Thank you very much, that was so kind of you" and secretly felt like a liar? For those who have, they end up feeling like a failure and a liar. The question for you is why do you downplay the compliment? Why do you lack that confidence and why are you so quick to dismiss it?

Is it because it's easier to agree and walk away? Even though you may live with the guilt later when you think about lying and how you wished you could have been honest. Why do you do that to yourself? Keep in mind you are by no means the only one who does this. I spent decades thinking that way. One of the main reasons we downplay compliments is because experience has taught us that we are ineffective, and whatever happened in that moment, whatever we did do, was not good enough. You thought the results were not meaningful and, therefore, you did not feel you were successful, you did not feel competence—so you lack confidence. Does that make sense?

The magic question

So what do you do about all this? How do you reconcile this often significant imbalance in your feelings of confidence and competence? You begin by understanding that the reason you, your child, and everyone else have low self-confidence is because of a critical step in building self-confidence that is missed. A step that people aren't even aware that they are taking. That single step is the question you subconsciously ask yourself to determine how effective you are at accomplishing your goals. And the way you answer that question is the difference between losing confidence and building it. That magic question is: "How am I doing?"

Each time you take action to make something happen, whether it is in school, work, relationships, sports, or whatever or wherever you are doing it, you are receiving some kind of feedback in some form that tells you how effective you are in accomplishing the outcome you set out to create. The feedback you receive gives you the information that allows you to answer the question, "How am I doing?"

Feedback

What examples can you think of that are sources of feedback in your life? How or where do you get feedback that lets you know how you are doing? People are a source of feedback. But we also live in an environment, a context, and we are talking about spectrumites with very sensitive nervous systems, right? Let's say you are a student in a school gymnasium. If it is one big echo chamber and you want to feel competent and confident in that space, you not only have people giving you feedback, you have echoing, squeaking sneakers that are beginning to disorganize you. Under these circumstances you are getting feedback that helps you feel incompetent in that space because of what it does to your nervous system. Does that make sense?

At work you may have a hard time concentrating when people are talking around you or the buzzing of the fluorescent lights is giving you a headache. I know how that feels. But in the case of people talking and an echoing gym, we've only addressed feedback in the form of sound. Some people have temperature sensitivities and going from a cold environment to a warm environment can be very disorganizing. Of course, if you feel disorganized, you do not feel focused, balanced, centered, and confident. You might feel very uneasy and like you can't pull yourself together because of the feedback you are getting from that environment.

You can also get feedback from "things." Those of you who are just as clumsy as I am may have had the experience of walking into a piece of furniture with your knee or little toe. When you do you get feedback from the "thing," or furniture, that you just hit. Perhaps you shout some colorful expletives as you feel the pain that answers the question, "How am I doing?" You were trying to cross the room gracefully, trying to get from Point A to Point B, but now you have walked into something. So, how do you answer the question, "How am I doing?" Maybe you will say, "Man, you klutz, what is wrong with you, don't you watch where you're going? What's your problem?"

What do you do to yourself when you use criticism to answer the question, "How am I doing?" Do you tear your confidence down or do you build it up? In that moment, in that single answer to that one question, you chose to reinforce a feeling of incompetence. In similar moments, we each have the opportunity to choose confidence or criticism. And this is the question that is always being asked and answered in the background of our minds all day long. Now, if you are on the spectrum, what kind of answers are you used to getting to the question, "How am I doing?" Primarily negative.

Spectrumites live on a steady diet of criticism. They get feedback repeating the messages that they aren't trying hard enough and aren't motivated. That they're being inappropriate and ultimately that they aren't good enough. So when they are answering the question, "How am I doing?" they have only that feedback as a point of reference.

Let's say they have sensory issues and are a little clumsy, or even a lot clumsy. Now they are trying to navigate their environment, tripping over their own feet. They are seeing everybody else handle loud noises while they are hypersensitive. So, how am I doing in this space? Well, "I'm weaker, I'm slower, and I'm not keeping up with things." That's how they are answering the question, "How am I doing?" They don't see themselves as effective, successful, creating meaningful results, so it is very difficult to see themselves as competent.

You need a different answer

How do we help our spectrum children and students to answer that question differently? We do it by setting them up for success every day of their lives. By facilitating the experience of competence in the simplest things. If a girl with fine motor difficulties finds it challenging to tie her shoes, then celebrate the success of putting her shoes on or getting up and getting dressed, feeding herself, or answering a question when it is asked. You can begin reinforcing any result a child creates with two simple words: "Thank you." You can reinforce it even more by thanking them for the specific result: "I really appreciate it when you did that for me because this is how it has helped me." Whenever you express your gratitude this specifically, it helps build her confidence with an understanding of the specific problems she's most effective at solving.

One person I shared this strategy with noted how many times a day we're asked the question "How are you doing?" as a greeting and lie about it. He said he tried answering the question honestly on several occasions when he wasn't doing well and those who asked the question didn't seem interested. But when he said things were good they would listen. The conclusion we drew, as you may have as well, is that when asked as a greeting, others may be surprised by an honest answer and not know how to respond. I, however, tend to answer the question honestly. I get frequent chuckles when I go through the drive-through at a fast food restaurant and when asked, "Hi, welcome, how are you today?" I respond, "I'm hungry." That's why I am there after all.

Thoughts on perfectionism

How do you help a child who is a perfectionist and becomes very upset with even the slightest mistake? My nine-year-old used to have that tendency when he helped cook. He loves helping in the kitchen and making his own scrambled eggs. In the past if he happened to drop something he would be very hard on himself. If we told him it was no big deal and he could clean it up, he'd become even more upset instead of reassured. The disconnect is that by the time we've told him it's no big deal, he's already answered the question "How am I doing?" negatively.

The key to repairing this disconnect and helping reduce his perfectionism is teaching him how to answer the question positively before the mistake ever happens. How the heck do you do that? By including the anticipation of accidents as part of the cooking process. When my son wants to cook, do I know accidents happen? Yes. When completing an assignment in class, do we know mistakes happen? Yes.

The problem is in the timing. We say, "Accidents happen" or "Mistakes are part of the process" *after* they've happened and *after* the child has answered the question. If the child is a perfectionist, then his belief is that mistakes aren't part of the process and they're simply not allowed. So your supportive comment that "accidents happen" is of little use other than to add to his frustration. Just like with my son.

Here's how you implement the strategy of answering the question positively beforehand. With my son, we discuss the process of cooking his eggs or whatever the project is. I ask him to explain the steps of the process to me as though he were teaching me. Several times throughout his explanation, I ask something like, "What if we drop an egg?" or "What if we spill something?" The answer is, "Then we clean it up." We then discuss how we'll clean it up. Now not only is a mistake anticipated but there's a solution for dealing with it when it does happen. He's clumsy like I am, so a mess will be made.

If the standard of meaningful results for him is to do it without making a mess, he'll probably have more discouraging experiences than confidence-building ones. But if the standard is being able to solve the problems inherent in the process, then success is his predominant experience.

Before I taught him to approach things this way, by doing it with him, his measure of success was avoiding mistakes. So when a mistake happened, it was seen as failure. Now that mistakes become part of the process and are seen at worst as more of an inconvenience than a disaster, we get to celebrate when things get dropped just as we planned so we can then implement our solution.

Let me give you another example. This same son has coordination issues and spills drinks at home and at restaurants frequently. He would become so embarrassed that he'd either start crying or run from the table and hide. The hiding caused an entirely new set of problems. So we applied the same strategy. After ordering drinks at the restaurant we'd ask, "What happens if it spills?" We'd plan the clean-up; then, if it happened, my wife or I would say, "Thank goodness we know how to solve this problem," and clean it up together.

It's important for us as adults to put our own reactivity in check and refrain from scolding a child for having a less than perfect moment. When you freak out you'll reinforce his tendency to be self-critical. Instead you simply acknowledge it and move into the solution by asking, "What do we do about it?" This approach has done wonders for his confidence.

Now he's at the point that if he spills something or drops something on the floor, he doesn't even look around to see if anybody is watching. He grabs a paper towel and a sponge and he just deals with it. That has become part of his process because he is not being called out every single time he does something less than perfect.

In our house, we do not draw negative attention to the human moments. Unfortunately, in other environments where people are looking for social appropriateness, they still criticize him for every little hiccup he has that deviates from the norm. I'm working on solving that problem by sharing this strategy with others.

This strategy goes beyond catching a child doing something right, such as, "Oh, good job, look how well you did that." The problem is that if your standard is that they must be doing something "right," how often does that actually happen? What if the rest of the time she did not do it quite right? What feedback do you give her then? Probably something along the lines of how it isn't right yet.

Grown-ups first

Negative feedback can come from those around us but let's not forget all of the negative feedback we give ourselves, especially as adults. We enter adulthood with a toolbox overflowing with various options for beating ourselves up. Have you ever had a hard day at work where you spent much of your eight-hour day getting nagged at by a colleague or chewed out by your boss? Then you get home and your kid wants to run to you and give you a hug? Then you find yourself uncomfortable with your child's positive energy or your spouse saying, "Glad you're home." In previous jobs, I had days like that where the confidence was kicked out of me and I just couldn't handle any more input, let alone a compliment. My kids, bless their hearts, are all waiting to see me with smiles and are glad I am home, but I cannot take compliments right then because it is very disproportionate to how I am feeling about me at the time.

So, when your child or anyone else rejects a compliment, it's because your compliment doesn't match her experience.

Experience, as we've been discussing, is the most powerful teacher. Is this making sense? If this sounds hard to apply, in all honesty it can be. Old habits die hard, don't they? This strategy requires a paradigm shift in your thinking, so spend some time with these ideas and change the way you answer the question for yourself before doing it with your child. Parents and teachers, you must go first. If you don't think this way, you won't naturally respond this way when supporting your children and students. If you continue to think in the old way, you'll be inconsistent at best with your child and that will make things worse because you'll be hypocritical and unreliable.

Another point about trying to build a child's confidence through positive feedback is this: Children don't learn well by being lectured. How many times have we tried to educate our children through a lecture? "Let me tell you what it was like, son. Let me tell you what is going to happen, missy, if you do not straighten up." A lecture does not teach. Experience does teach, and never more so than when it comes to confidence. That is why it is so important. I imagine you can recall the times you'd tune your parents out whenever the lecture would start. Your children and students are doing the same thing.

Not good enough

Here are more thoughts on how to address perfectionism in our children. Why do you think many of our kids seek perfection? In my experience, it's because the state of perfection is the state where mistakes do not exist. It means you have done everything right. So, these kids who are used to having the criticism piled on all day, every day, think that if they achieve perfection, they will not receive any criticism. Of course, we know perfection is unachievable. But these are kids who are told, "We all make mistakes," and aren't comforted, because in their experience it seems that all they do is make mistakes and that nothing is ever good enough. Even when they do it well, someone always wants them to do it better, faster, more efficiently, more legibly.

There is always feedback that no matter what they do, it is not good enough. So, on the one hand, we say to our kids, "Be yourself, believe in who you are, try your best," but when they do that, what's the feedback? How do you address the "How am I doing?" question? You say, "Well, you can do better," or "See how well you have done—well, guess what, you can do even better." So, as much as we think we are encouraging our children, we are still answering that question for them that it is just not good enough yet. And you will also see that when kids make a simple mistake and they go over the top with their reaction, beating themselves up, it's because they now have to hear their inner critic answer the question "How am I doing?" with statements of how incompetent they feel.

Consider this. Maybe perfectionism isn't a tendency of someone who is on the spectrum. Maybe perfectionism is the result of a negative self-concept acquired in response to feedback from the environment that is overly negative and that the child eventually internalizes. Does this make sense?

I believe that OCD, or obsessive-compulsive disorder, can be thought of as perfectionism in action. Wanting to control your environment and wanting to make it perfect. Perfectionism in yourself is when you want to do things right and meticulously and want to be right all of the time. OCD is another expression of that. Having a perfect arrangement in an environment—if you can't control yourself and can't be perfect yourself, you aspire to make your environment perfect or make your rituals perfect. But it all comes down to the same thing. These are kids who want to feel competent, feel effective, and feel like they are creating meaningful results and that is how they go about it.

Emphasize where they specialize

This strategy can be particularly difficult for teachers to implement because they are entrusted with skill building. They must give feedback to their students on how to improve existing skills and often have to compete with a child's inner critic that filters that feedback negatively. When it comes to working with children on the spectrum, you may encounter the child that excels academically and the child that struggles in every subject.

The important thing to focus on when giving feedback in an area a child consistently struggles in is whether it is one of his areas of strength. Is he good at it? Is it his specialty? As with every spectrumite my skill-set is very disproportionate. Though I am very articulate with well-developed verbal and written communication, I have dyspraxia, which means I have gross motor clumsiness and I trip over my own feet. I need to look at the ground when I walk to keep my balance because if I look straight ahead or to the side while moving I will start to tip and teeter. I have touch, light, and hearing sensitivities. I have dysgraphia, difficulty in writing. It is painful for me to sign my name on a check. So, when people hear me speak confidently, they often assume I have generalized confidence and competence, which is not the case.

I have heard many educators, as well as some parents, make the assertion that because a child is smart in one area, she should not have any issues in other areas. Well, yes, she is smart in her area of specialization because spectrumites are specialized human beings. Most neurotypicals are generalists; spectrumites are specialists. The frustration we have in a school setting is we are expected to be generalists because that is the rule of the school.

So here's one value you need to have as a teacher even though some of you may throw up your hands in disgust over the mere suggestion of it. Appreciate the child for her specialization and nurture that. Let go of the areas that will cause the child nothing but frustration and the repeated experience of incompetence, such as the tripod grip on the pencil and meticulous punctuation, at the expense of being able to express her needs and wants in writing. I know you have government-mandated testing standards that need to be met, and what a source of daily frustration that is for you as an educator. We both know that no test score is more important than the self-concept of a child, so you need to negotiate how you approach the task with that child.

I personally cannot spell worth a darn and neither can my father, who raised four kids, running his own business, which by the way was built on his mechanical genius and didn't require spelling. He did it with strong support from my mother, who has a complementary skill-set. He is proof that spectrumites find a way to navigate the world using their strengths but only when their strengths are nurtured and shaped into something they and the world can use. It is more important to teach our children how to collaborate with people who have skills that complement their own, instead of trying to force skills that cause them psychological or physical pain to perform.

I have difficulty structuring a sentence in writing. I found people who help me correct that; they edit for me. I have difficulty with any mathematical calculation that requires me to count beyond ten fingers. I barely made it through math class. Algebra—you might as well have given me a root canal without sedation.

Think about it in terms of negotiating the middle ground—what is absolutely necessary to meet the needs of your requirements as a teacher but also the child's need for competence. I understand that the teachers are in a difficult place here. They are held accountable for the test scores. They are in as much of a win–lose situation as the student ends up being put in, and that unfortunately is a sin of the system. That is something that is broken and needs to be made more flexible. I know I am preaching to the choir here, and I know there are parents and teachers who would like a little bit more flexibility so they could teach to the needs of the individual, but unfortunately the system does not currently allow for that. But we are working on it. We will get there because I know we are all committed to it.

Constructive criticism

There is something out there that I have heard parents say that children need to learn how to take and that is, constructive criticism. Are there any bigger oxymorons than that? Constructive criticism—what do you think of that term? What, if any, issues do you have with the term *constructive criticism*?

I think of constructive criticism as well-intended negative feedback. It is like someone calling someone a fat slob and then saying they don't mean it in a bad way. You are basically trying to cover up an insult. So, what is the alternative? Constructive criticism to most people is thought of as a means of giving guidance for improving upon what could be done better. Is this accurate?

The problem with constructive criticism is it comes out as, "Here is what you are doing wrong, and here is how to do it better." You are leading with a negative or leading in with the fault. So here's the alternative I use with my own children and teach to my clients as well. This is one of my best strategies. You can eliminate the criticism altogether, and the tendency for the person to take it personally, by offering feedback about how the situation is going instead of how the person is doing. Here's how it would sound:

You approach a child who is having difficulty and instead of asking, "Are you having a problem?" you instead ask, "Is something not working?" Now a child who is used to hearing criticism will initially hear it as personal and may respond with something like, "I'm fine, I don't need any help." But remember, with this approach, you're not asking about the child, you're asking about the aspect of the situation that isn't working. So when the child says, "I'm fine, I don't need any help," you respond, "Oh, I'm sure you're doing fine. I was wondering if something in this situation wasn't going the way it needs to go." This small adjustment can take the responsibility or the fault away from the child and make it about the situation. It is much easier for the child to hear feedback when the negative is not aimed at him. You want to build confidence and build opportunities for problem solving. But the moment you say there is a problem and that he or she caused the problem, the child does not want any more feedback from you.

One parent asked how a child could be taught responsibility without constructive criticism. First realize that feedback given with a tone of blame and fault finding only teaches shame. Emphasizing the situation teaches a child that her relationship with the situation is a factor in the problem, and that by changing her approach, she can create a better outcome. But when the feedback is about the child, it places the entire fault on her.

A mother shared the following story with me. Her son (who is on the spectrum) is involved in a baseball league. In a recent game he hit the winning run, and it was the only run in the game. They took pictures and were very celebratory. When she talked to him about it later that day he acted like it was no big deal. A few days later when she showed him the pictures, one of them was when he actually hit the ball and that was the winning run. It was then that he smiled and accepted the compliment. This is a testament to the overall theme of this chapter that experience has greater credibility than words alone. In this instance, the excitement of the moment may have made it difficult for this young man to process the contribution he'd made to his team. But with time and the concrete proof provided by the photo he was able to believe it.

I hope that you understand the power that lies in the moment you ask and answer the question "How am I doing?" It can mean the difference between seeing yourself as someone who solves problems and someone who is the problem.

The more you and your child learn to see yourselves as people who solve problems, the faster you'll be able to bounce back and keep moving forward. We all know that the social world can sometimes be brutal and unforgiving, but it can also be empowering and filled with joy and opportunities.

Mastering how you answer this question is key to the success of every relationship you'll ever have, especially the one with yourself. Until you can master how you receive feedback, it is difficult to even engage another human being. Since you have come this far in this book and are committed to applying what you've learned so far, I encourage you to answer this question the same way I am: How am I doing? I'm doing beautifully.

How praise can ruin your child's life

I want to finish this chapter with an example of how even the best feedback can unknowingly have the opposite effect. If you have ever raised a teenager you know what a hormone-fueled, supercharged rollercoaster ride of emotional reactivity it can be. Now throw in autism and it's like giving a pyromaniac a box of matches to play with in a room full of high explosives.

My thirteen-year-old spectrumite has had a glorious transition from a special needs school to public middle school (his choice) and exceeded everyone's expectations in terms of keeping up with the increased course load and managing the chaos of changing classes with loud crowded hallways, or so we thought.

About five months into the school year his attitude began deteriorating. He was becoming more moody, bossy to his brothers, and increasingly isolated. He became inflexibly obsessed with a new video game system and seemingly more depressed each time we told him we wouldn't give him the money to purchase it.

You may be asking, "So what's unusual about a spectrumite being moody and obsessed with video games?" What's different is that it intensified in a short time, and he was unable to bounce back from being told "No" as he's been able to in the past. Instead he sank even lower. One night his emotions peaked and I found him at bedtime curled up in tears after having locked himself in his room for several hours. In the past he'd stay in his room for long periods to cool off, after which he'd be fine.

This time he was so distraught that it was difficult getting him to talk about what was upsetting him so much. He kept saying that no one understood him, even me. This was a shocking statement as he typically refers to me as the only person who does understand.

He repeatedly said, "No one knows how to work with me," "No one understands me," "I'm confused about school, life and everything." He shook more and more as he talked and I wasn't sure where this would lead but I prepared myself for a long night. I can't remember exactly how the dialogue went but I concentrated on his every word to look for clues.

I mentioned to him that he repeated the words "nobody," "everyone," "24/7," and other all-or-nothing phrases that created a perception of complete isolation from anything or anyone that was working for him. I explored with him the things he felt "no one" was getting or helping with and what he absolutely needed them to know and understand. I asked him this question being fully prepared to in no way minimize whatever statement came out of his mouth. I was asking him to trust me to be an exception to his "nobody" belief and I wasn't going to blow it.

When I was finally able to reassure him that it was him and me, that he wasn't alone, and we would find a solution, he finally opened up about what was upsetting him. He said he really enjoyed the teachers and the classes but the busy halls and all the students were too much for him to handle.

He had moved from a school in which he moved between two classrooms with a total of maybe ten students, to a school of about one thousand students in which he was in (I think) ten different class periods, with up to thirty-six kids in a class and so on.

He had appeared unfazed in navigating this new environment. With all of my sensory sensitivities and what I knew of his, I had no idea how he was doing it. So I asked him why he had been keeping this to himself for so long. Please note this following statement because it is critical for you to understand. He said, *"Everyone was so proud of me that I didn't want to disappoint you."* I felt the energy drain out of me when he said that, as I felt I might have sent a signal to him I never meant to send. So I told him, "I want you to know that I'm deeply sorry if I ever gave you the impression that my being proud of you was something you had to earn."

I added that each time he asked more of himself I was proud of him because he took that step. I let him know that the step was what was important. Not every step is going to give us the result we want. Many teach us that the step we took is one that we don't want to repeat, while others leave us grateful we did. It's the courage he showed in taking the step that made me proud of him.

Further discussion revealed that:

1. He believed he'd be sent back to the special needs school if he didn't adjust perfectly to the middle school.

2. Each time he succeeded, I, my wife and school staff told him how proud they were of him. He believed the pride to be attached to the accomplishment and thought that if he discovered it wasn't working and wanted to change it then the pride would vanish.

3. He also kept taking on more responsibilities and joining more clubs so he could keep hearing, "I'm proud of you." He did this until he couldn't do it anymore.

4. Regarding his obsession with the video game, the computer, etc. (all of which he'd been grounded from because of the way he was acting), he revealed that these were the methods he used to drown out the negative thoughts he was having about how bad he felt. Taking them away removed his coping mechanism, which escalated things. However, if we hadn't taken them away, who knows if and when the truth would have bubbled to the surface.

His ability to sustain himself in this win–lose situation deteriorated. I really have to hand it to the staff that work with him on a daily basis and have consistently been there for him. He said, "The teachers and counselors are the reason I don't freak out every day."

We discussed how the middle school was about him getting an education; it wasn't about tolerating noisy, crowded hallways and dealing with jerks at the lunchroom table. Neither of those were measures of success.

As he began to settle down I asked him if he felt calmer and he said, "Yes." I asked him if he understood things differently. He talked about how he realized things seemed different when he talked about them instead of keeping them in. Essentially, putting words to his experience helped make it more clear so it could be examined and thought through.

Once he was smiling again and ready to go to bed I asked him what he learned from our discussion. He said, "To do what makes me happy." I added, "It's also important that you never feel you are responsible for making yourself unhappy in order to make others happy." Things have been so much better ever since.

Chapter 8

Meeting Halfway

The greatest challenge in forming relationships with spectrumites is resolving the often radically different communication styles between you. I'm not referring to simple differences in style, but more importantly to differences in the spectrum brain that affect how information is communicated and interpreted.

My middle son, for example, has both expressive and receptive language issues. The term *expressive* refers to the ability to getting the words out and *receptive* refers to understanding the information coming in. Imagine how challenging life can be when you have difficulty communicating in one direction, let alone both.

Those with these language issues are extremely frustrated as interactions with others are fraught with miscommunications and misunderstandings as the norm instead of the exception. Others mistakenly refer to these spectrumites as defiant, stubborn and worse, when in reality they are experiencing a significant communication breakdown.

Be curious

People on the outside looking in see behavior when what they are not asking themselves is, "Why is this? Of all the things this child could do to engage his world, why this? When it gets them negative feedback, why this?" You must view what a child does through the eyes of curiosity instead of judgment.

A tendency of the human mind is that once it decides it's right, it wants to stay that way because people need certainty in their lives. But when it comes to our kids, you need to begin by requiring yourself to get facts to back up your conclusions. When you instead rely on your assumptions or best guess you do both yourself and the child a tremendous injustice.

At the very least, a spectrumite does what he does because a huge communication breakdown has occurred due to the way he uses feedback. In many cases, it's a misinterpretation of feedback; in other cases, he may not even know that feedback exists. Once you and he find out what the missing pieces are or where the disconnect is, you can act to put those pieces in place. It can make all the difference in the world.

Expressive and receptive language issues can present as delays in responding and understanding what is being asked of you. So allowing him a little more time to respond is an important first step. In some cases a spectrumite may need a few days to think about a question before responding, especially when it pertains to a problem he's having. Otherwise, requesting an immediate response could result in him shutting down, or having an anxiety attack.

Keep an open mind

Though you understand the value of adjusting your communication style to accommodate his style, the general population tends to be inflexible in their approach and want it done their way.

Consider the reality of many on the spectrum who are nonverbal, or unable to communicate through spoken language. Perhaps they learn sign language or use a communication device with a keyboard instead. The important thing is to identify the means of communication that works best for him and work with the school system to help actively integrate it into their school experience, especially in their interactions with teachers and students.

The fact is that communication needs to be flexible. So many people insist upon the spoken word, and for some on the spectrum, it is simply too difficult to create. Look at another group of people in the special needs population—people who are born deaf. They may be unable to speak, yet they have sign language as an option. For some reason, that is allowed for those who can't hear, but for some children with speech delays or challenges, that same privilege is often denied them. I'm not saying give up on teaching verbal communication—my middle son had a significant speech delay and has come a long way with the help of speech therapists. He still has difficulty speaking, but it is far easier to understand him now and he is much better able to self-advocate as a result. I'm saying it is critical to keep an open mind about what it means to communicate.

Why social skills groups don't work

For years my clients on the spectrum have been telling me why the social skills groups their parents send them to simply don't work. Recently a young mother shared her frustration with me. She said the only thing her son (with Asperger's) learned was how to be a robot. He learned to ask questions like, "How was your weekend?" in a mechanical way but nothing about how to connect with people.

Many more parents are figuring this out as well; however, many continue to send their kids to such groups because they don't know what else to do (we'll get into that) and they're hoping that something will sink in if they keep sending their kids. Part of the problem is that their kids are afraid to give them honest feedback about the groups because it's met with anger from their parents. I've heard many parents tell me that these groups did wonders for their child. That is until I spoke to the child.

Here's what I've learned over the years from my clients and the reasons why I no longer offer or refer people to social skills groups.

Reason 1: Time and place

- Social skills groups are often held after school when a child is overloaded from the school day, or on a Saturday when a child needs downtime.

- They also often take place in a crowded, noisy room that disorganizes children, exhausts them, and yet is a room in which they are expected to learn.

Reason 2: Fake it until the adults get off your back

- Spectrumites of elementary school through high school age have explained that they do what they need to do in these groups to avoid criticism and get their parents off their backs. Once they've done enough "performing" to make the adults happy enough to stop sending them to these groups they slowly slide back into their comfort zone.

- One young man told me in front of his mother that he pretended to like the group, because if he was honest she'd lecture him about how he's not trying hard enough, giving it a chance, or how she'll shop around until she finds one that works. His solution was to make her happy instead of getting his own needs met.

Reason 3: It doesn't happen this way

- These groups are facilitated in a way that bears no resemblance to any social situation its attendees will have outside of the group. Did you learn to socialize in a conference room with one or more adults using a white board to explain relationships like a lesson from a social studies textbook? Adults who, by the way, don't understand what it's like to be you?

- Who said the way to learn social skills is in a room full of people you didn't choose to work with, led by a person focused on fun activities intended to teach, but who might sometimes forget to explain to the kids what they're supposed to be learning? Some also don't take the time to determine if the kids actually care.

- It doesn't matter that they *should care*, you can only teach them when they *do care*

Reason 4: Where are the parents?

- This point is crucial to understand. Social skills groups tend to focus on the relationships you want to have when they need to focus on the relationships you already have.

- The people most motivated to help you succeed in your relationships are your family members and where are they? In the waiting room. Learning to have relationships with a peer group that is looking for any opportunity to pounce is a recipe for failure.

- The relationships that are the foundation of learning meaningful, sustainable, and generalizable social strategies are the ones these children experience every day, not the occasional ones that occur in a group setting.

Reason 5: The bribe

- Almost one hundred percent of the spectrumites I spoke to were either bribed or threatened into going to group sessions. Anything from a promise of a new video game, a favorite meal, or the threat of being denied things was common. The group itself and the intended benefits of it were a secondary concern.

- The child learned that the requirement was showing up, dealing with it and then the reward would be given or the consequence would be avoided. Does this sound like a recipe for success to you?

Reason 6: Learning should be part of everyday life

- How often do these groups meet? Maybe an hour once a week? What good is that? Learning and applying social strategies needs to be something that is the focus of your everyday life, not the subject of a one-hour-a-week class that goes by so fast you wonder what the point is.

Reason 7: Repeat after me

- One child explained to his father that in his group they spent the whole time following the "When I say this, you say that" guide to social success. The father was surprised and admitted he didn't ask for details about what went on in the classes. He trusted the clinician (after all, why would you offer such a class unless you were qualified?)

- He was also used to his son telling him what he wanted to hear because he wanted his father to be happy with him instead of disappointed once again.

Reason 8: Osmosis

- There is a myth in this world that children on the spectrum will learn socialization simply by having the opportunity to socialize. Wrong! That's how neurotypical kids learn, because they're wired to pick up the feedback they get from those they're interacting with.

- People on the spectrum don't learn this way, that's why they're on the spectrum.

What the heck does a parent do now?

Spectrumites learn best one on one when there are fewer distractions, more quality control and less risk than that posed by looking bad in front of a room full of strangers in which relationship skills are taught by rote, assembly line fashion.

What I have experienced in my own life and have been teaching parents for years now is how to identify and maximize the number of teachable moments in the lives of their children. The moments that have actual meaning for them occur in the relationships they currently have. The ones who need the training are the parents. Placing all of the pressures on the spectrumite to make a relationship work is ignorant and cruel. They need a partner who is learning with them and conspiring for their success.

I find the best success when parents and their children work together and improve their own relationship first. Those experiences are far more meaningful and generalizable than the "read, remember, and regurgitate" style that exists in far too many social skills groups today.

I want to make it clear that I'm not against teaching spectrumites social strategies in a group setting. In fact, I find that spectrumites tend to benefit more from support groups than social skills groups. In a support group they're allowed to sit and listen which gives them time to identify who they can connect with. It also gives them time to introspect and build their self-awareness as they listen to others put language to their experiences.

When I ran support groups it was a frequent experience for members to become excited when hearing their experiences validated and even the quietest members of the group would begin opening up and asking for advice. They wanted the guidance, when they saw those who understood were giving it.

Unfortunately, many parents and professionals believe that something is better than nothing. This is a dangerous approach because if the something only serves the purpose of reinforcing to your child that yet again, something didn't work, and once more he's asked to do something that isn't a good fit, this just reinforces the experience that socialization equals pain.

I recommend taking a step back and evaluating the time, effort, expense and aggravation that goes into compelling him to engage with one of these groups. If you find that what keeps you going isn't the results you experience but is more the anticipation of results "someday," then it's time to regroup.

Seek out those who can teach you how to authentically connect with your spectrumite in a way that teaches him how to have a relationship with you. A relationship isn't about the mechanics of conversation; it is about the partnership of two people. Once we learn how to create one successful partnership, we then have the tools to create others.

Be true to yourself

It is of critical importance that spectrumites remain true to ourselves and yet get the tools we need to effectively engage the world. If you have ever included your child in social skills classes, what has been your experience in terms of the measure of success for these groups? As it turns out, opinions on what successful social skills are varies from group to group. The skills I hear most commonly emphasized are eye contact, being able to greet somebody when you meet them, and "chitchatty" types of conversations. I have been able to accomplish a lot, and yes, I am very verbal and very articulate, but when it comes to nonverbal communication, I miss about eighty percent of it so I have learned to compensate for the fact that there is a lot of information coming in that I don't see.

In my opinion, teaching spectrum kids to read nonverbal communication is as practical as teaching a blind person how to navigate a sightseeing tour. It makes more sense to teach them what they're missing and how to get it using the strengths they have. People who are blind read through touch using Braille, or through hearing using audio books. I am verbal and ask a lot of questions. So I use that strength to ask the questions most effective at getting the information I need.

A few of my clients who have difficulty finding the words to speak communicate better through texting than speaking, so those who allow them that option in their relationships are able to understand them better and have a closer relationship with them. It's all about doing what's necessary instead of doing what's common.

My greatest frustration with the social skills classes of my experience is their insistence on trying to get our kids to make their brains do things that their brains do not do—recognize nonverbal communication, recognize vocal tone, recognize body posture and body language. If your brain does not pick that stuff up, you cannot make it. People have told me my entire life that I need to look at body language, expression, and look at this, look at that. Guess what? It doesn't work and I will explain to you the reasons why that is and what you can do about it. Just because you cannot spot nonverbal communication does not mean you can't get that information somehow. I will go into that, too.

Communication is basically about giving and receiving feedback about how we're doing in our relationships. How effective am I? Am I getting it right? Am I upsetting anybody? Am I messing things up? And for kids on the spectrum, the question "How am I doing?" is often answered resoundingly with criticism: "You are doing it wrong, you're being inappropriate, you need to stop that or do that differently." No wonder our confidence ends up in the toilet.

How are spectrumites supposed to remember rules that don't match their experience of the world? Through memorization, using scripts? Relationships don't work like that. If they're mechanical, then all you're doing is acting when you need to be connecting. When this person does this, you are supposed to do that. Well, guess what? Life is not scripted, folks. We do not learn that way. We learn by thinking, understanding, and having beliefs and values that inform the way we communicate because rote memorization does not teach.

I received a great question from a mother recently who was trying to teach her spectrum son to socialize and asked, "How am I supposed to teach him how to socialize when I don't know how I learned it? I just got it." And I think that pretty much sums it all up because the neurotypicals of the world learn through osmosis—they watch other people, catch the facial expressions, detect patterns, and through trial and experience, they learn how to adjust what they do.

But people on the spectrum miss the majority of information needed to know what adjustments are needed. As I mentioned earlier, I hear a lot about social skills classes from my clients, and rarely does anyone report learning anything they can use. I have heard of different models out there that people say have had resounding success, and which have benefited their child, so I am not going to discount the idea that some can be effective, but unfortunately there are more that are not effective.

Strategy versus skill

Spectrumites need to learn strategies, not just skills. We hear about social skills classes—what is a skill? A skill is a technique. A strategy is how you use that skill to solve a problem. That is a fundamental difference. It is not just about shaking a person's hand or making eye contact. The strategy is, how do you do it, why do you do it, and what problem does it solve for you and the person you're relating to? That is what a strategy is. It is far more complex. Skills are not enough, which is why I focus on teaching strategies.

Let me give you a real-world example: Dribbling a basketball is a skill. You can stand in place and dribble a basketball. But being able to dribble a basketball up and down a basketball court during an intense, loud, fast-moving game requires a strategy. Does that make sense?

When you think about how the typical social skills group is run, it tends to be in close-to-ideal circumstances that exclude the sensory assaults that our children must face when they go out into the world. So, if you are going to teach your kids, teach them in the very context they are going to have to be effective in, because then they'll encounter the problems they need to solve in that space to be effective communicators. I'm not suggesting you saturate them to the point of a meltdown, only that you have them practice the strategies in the environments they'll ultimately need to apply them in.

One rule about any strategy is that it is only as useful as the problem it solves. If it causes problems, it is not useful and spectrumites will resist it. So, if making eye contact causes them problems, they are not going to want to do it. You think it'll solve a problem for the rest of the world because they are used to eye contact, but if it causes a problem for a spectrumite and you have not addressed that and taught her how to solve it, then socialization can become a source of pain.

Of course that is not what you want for your children. You try to teach them to be effective socializers and communicators, but you risk also teaching them that they must be in pain to do so. If you want them to engage the world, don't make them afraid of it. Besides, there are strategies to get around that. If people are used to those things as part of socializing, then we need strategies for managing those expectations. You can inform the other person how you socialize. If you let people know how to talk to you that can solve a lot of problems.

What if social skills classes weren't just about insisting you adopt behaviors people supposedly expect and how to perform them? What if, instead, they emphasized understanding how people tend to communicate? Then you could begin devising strategies that allow you to communicate in a way that allows you to dispense with what's ordinarily expected and yet allows you to still communicate effectively. Wouldn't that be a practical happy medium? What do you think?

Solving the problem

Strategies are designed to solve problems. But before you can use them there are a few things you need to know:

1. If you are looking to solve the problem, you need to know when the problem exists. Well, if you have difficulty taking in feedback, you may not accept the information that tells you something isn't working. However, when you learn to accept such feedback you can identify when problems exist and then determine which strategy to learn and implement in order to solve them.

2. You need to care about the problem and be interested in solving it.

3. You need to know how to apply the strategy to solve it.

4. You need to know when the problem has been solved. All those steps are critical in being able to apply a strategy.

How effective are spectrumites typically when it comes to problem solving? They're pretty ineffective unless it's in the area of their special interest. Social problem solving is the greatest area of challenge, as one mother points out, "My son doesn't often know that there is a problem. For instance, he's playing in the neighborhood with his peers, and they are all roughhousing and having a great old time, but then they send up that invisible social cue that they are done. He will go in for one last wrestle or one last punch because that is what everybody has been doing, but now he is in trouble because everyone else was done. Then everybody will tell him to go home, and there are tears and he doesn't understand why he was sent home or what the problem was and he doesn't even realize there was a problem."

In exploring this further it turns out that none of his peers told him what the problem was. They simply became angry with him for it and sent him away. This happened to me often. When it comes to the unspoken cue he probably missed he needs a means of knowing when the game is over, a concrete way of knowing. When you try to teach abstract concepts like meanings, innuendo, etc., for a concrete mind, these can be very elusive. So to have strategies that are far more concrete and measurable makes it easier for a concrete thinker to be socially effective. A strategy is also deliberate, goal-oriented, and you use it in order to create a specific measurable result. Like when you shoot a basketball in a specific way, you know how it is going to go in the basket. When you are playing football and you execute a previously practiced pattern to get a touchdown and it works, it is concrete and measurable.

Leaving things open ended and asking someone to go with the flow provides no goal and sense of what strategy to apply. It's like going out driving without a map. There is no way to navigate a situation if the expectation is to go with the flow.

Another critical point about strategies is that they are not based on what's appropriate. They are based on what's effective. Appropriate is subjective and always changing; it isn't measurable. Is it any wonder that our kids are always being told they are inappropriate, and need to be acting more appropriately? How can you accomplish being "appropriate" when you can't define it? There is no cause and effect in "appropriate." So, let's focus on being effective because the root word of effective is *effect*—cause and effect—what is the problem, what is the solution? That's what a strategy does, so it is important to teach our kids to think strategically.

Referring back to what I said earlier about certain expectations causing problems for me such as making eye contact and shaking hands: To prevent or minimize painful social interactions, I need strategies to solve the problems caused by doing either of those two things. Without those strategies, I stand to lose more than I gain from interacting with others. For instance, when I am giving presentations and people want to walk up and shake my hand, I am so hypersensitive to touch that if I shake too many hands, I get close to overload before I even start presenting. Fortunately, in that setting, I can disclose this sensitivity to people and they respect it.

The reason handshakes are so uncomfortable is because people use different grips when they shake hands, and hands have different textures—some soft, rough, slimy; some grip too hard, too loose—and my mind is processing all of that information. It's too much touch and too much variety. It's overwhelming. If I am told it is appropriate to shake hands and I put myself in a situation where I have to shake too many, I will lose every single time just to make other people happy, and that is not reasonable. So, it is important to keep in mind that, when you are teaching your child any kind of a skill or strategy, it is imperative that you understand and ask yourself the question: Am I causing him problems or solving his problems by encouraging him to use this strategy?

It is important for you to realize that doing what you're supposed to do when you're supposed to do it is not always simple. Socialization and communication have to solve more problems than they cause, plain and simple. The way to help make this happen is through strategies that make socialization more concrete, less threatening, and more flexible, so spectrumites do not have to do all the work and force themselves to engage in what they clearly are not good at just to make other people happy.

What you believe

Has your child ever resisted being taught a strategy? One of the main reasons for the resistance is that she doesn't believe her life is going to improve if she learns it. A strategy that will help her be more socially appropriate while also causing her to feel more uncomfortable doesn't make sense. Give her credit for having the intelligence and self-awareness to know there is potential harm in what is being asked of her.

Another belief that can sabotage learning a new strategy is the belief that it is important to be right. It is of little value to explain to your child that he doesn't have to be right all of the time; that sometimes it's OK to be wrong. When you do so all you're doing is telling him what your belief is without acknowledging what his belief is. His belief, of course, is that it is important to be right and his behavior is an extension of it. So, if you want to teach him a new strategy for listening to another person's point of view you need to start by changing the belief that it is important to be right.

It's not going to work to teach him, when a person does this, you do this, when a person says this, you say that. You are not going to influence his belief. If he doesn't have a belief to support using the new strategy there is no logic in using it. Unfortunately, a lot of social trainings do not address the child's belief system. They mistakenly think that socialization is only a skill-set.

Social communication is actually a complex set of processes that involve assessing a situation, knowing when the problem exists, deciding what problems in that situation you need to prioritize, determining what the solution is, and implementing the solution.

It's contextual

One mother discussed the challenges she has getting her son to behave at the mall. Though she explained the rules to him, he would end up bumping into people as though they weren't there, he would yell at her when she would redirect him, and more. What she didn't realize is that the mall isn't just about interacting with people; it is about being in that space. If there are sensory issues in that environment that cause problems he can't solve, then as long as he has those problems, there is no way he is going to socialize effectively. With all those problems happening at once that are probably overwhelming him, she was expecting him to remember, prioritize and execute polite social protocols. Does that sound like a reasonable request to make of him?

That is why so many spectrumites like one-on-one, quiet environments where we are not being multitasked. It is easier to prioritize and focus on the art and strategy of socialization because we are able to prioritize and focus on only a few things. Imagine trying to socialize when you have executive functioning challenges that make it difficult to focus, avoid distraction, manage your anxiety and multitask?

Imagine what it's like in a mall, cafeteria, classroom, office or group of people. We are asked to socialize in the very settings where we're least likely to be effective and most likely to feel incompetent when we try. That's why I emphasize teaching your child to socialize in one-on-one relationships with yourselves and siblings in settings that aren't so demanding. Then when she's confident in her social effectiveness you can gradually introduce her to environments that make it difficult, identify exactly what makes it difficult and solve those problems. A simple example is wearing earplugs in a restaurant so you can hear the person in front of you without having to work so hard to tune out the noise around you. Does that make sense?

This is why I won't go to a party, a mall, a church, or any other place that disorganizes me. It is difficult for me to focus on anything because I am restless, agitated and nervous. If I stay in that disorganized state long enough, I become angry, and that ends up causing me more problems than it solves. So, making myself socialize in those environments does not make sense.

I mentioned before that executive functioning issues make it extremely challenging to communicate and socialize; difficult but not impossible. What you need is the happy medium. If people in your life enjoy parties and restaurants, then arrange get-togethers with fewer people. There is absolutely nothing that requires you to socialize in sensory chaos. Take turns having each other over for dinner instead of going out, or at least choose restaurants that have quiet areas. I'm a fan of brunch and lupper (the latter being a meal that falls between lunch and supper). The in-between hours before the crowds hit. It makes for a more enjoyable time when you like to get out of the house and still avoid the sensory assaults of that environment.

Ultimately, it is a matter of doing what is necessary for you and whoever you are with, to find a common way of communicating with each other in order to maximize understanding between the two of you. Meet each other halfway.

Chapter 9

Clarify, Clarify, Clarify

If you accept one thing about social communication it needs to be this: People on the autism spectrum are not designed to read nonverbal language, and insisting that we decode it is as unreasonable as making a color-blind person distinguish between red, green, and blue. Our brains don't do it. They don't decode nonverbal information, and yet the reality is that this information is out there and people are using it to communicate with us. We miss things and we always will. So, what do we do about that? We will get into that shortly.

I, for one, miss a lot of facial expressions and physical mannerisms. I could either put all the pressure on myself to figure out what a person means by what he is doing, like social skills training tells me I'm supposed to. Doing so, by the way, also denies the person I'm talking to the responsibility of having to speak up and explain himself better instead. This is the pressure that is put on spectrumites when you say, "OK, now watch their facial expressions. What does that mean? What is this nonverbal cue telling you?"

Imagine being put under that kind of pressure to focus on all the things that you don't understand, that your brain doesn't pick up, instead of learning how to use other strategies to compensate that don't require you to fight your own brain and that still allow you to get the same information. I have figured out ways to get the information I miss visually in an auditory way because that's how I primarily experience the world.

The expectation of most social skills training is that people on the spectrum need to be able to read nonverbal communication, know what it means, and adjust what they say and do accordingly. My question is this: Why don't we teach them that their primary strategy needs to be knowing that nonverbal communication exists, that it transmits information, and how to ask questions in order to encourage a person to verbalize or in some other concrete way express what they're communicating nonverbally? In fact, it is fair to refer to my system of communication as one that operates as though nonverbal communication didn't exist. How exactly do you teach someone to do that?

No mind reading

The fact is I teach it to my clients every day, and it's extremely effective. Now, in the past, others have responded to this suggestion by saying that their son or daughter asks a lot of questions already and are often perceived as being rude. I'm talking about asking questions strategically, based on the conscious knowledge of what you need to know to increase the understanding between yourself and others. So any old question won't do; it needs to be more focused and deliberate. Understand the difference?

Besides, a verbal response provides far more concrete feedback than nonverbal communication ever will. Of course, we need to learn how to ask questions without being rude. Questions to help us know what other people are thinking, how we are being perceived, and make statements that share how we perceive them. Under no circumstances is one person required to guess what the other person is thinking. Always ask.

Now let's define a few terms here before I reveal what I consider the most import social strategy there is. The first term is *communication*: It is a process of sharing information using an agreed-upon method such as speaking, writing, texting, e-mailing, or signing. And it is following agreed-upon rules of exchange.

The agreement may result in one person using verbal communication while the other uses a talking board. They have agreed to communicate that way, and they have agreed upon rules of exchange. Do our rules allow us to "trash talk" like some of the guys in the gym? Are we allowed to tease each other? Or are we respectful? You agree on how to do that, too. That also eliminates a lot of misunderstandings such as, "What do you mean by that, why did you do that?" Well, you need to agree on how to talk to each other. I have clients with whom one person verbally asks a question and the person on the spectrum picks up her cell phone and texts a response because, for her, it is much easier to find language that way.

Many of my clients become very disorganized when there's a lot of emotion in a conversation, which then makes speech more difficult to produce. Having the option to text or e-mail is the solution to that problem. You see, even though you know what the words are in your mind, if you're too disorganized, you often can't get your mouth to cooperate. I have had this experience many times.

A pet peeve I have is an approach often utilized in the school system in which a child who is upset is encouraged to "use your words." When a spectrumite is upset to the point that her mouth won't work and the only option you give her to communicate with you is to speak, you will escalate her distress or cause her to shut down. Asking her to "use your words" also makes one thing very clear: You don't get it. Your role under those circumstances is to be present with her, let her calm down until she's organized enough to find the language, and then you have the conversation.

Before I share what I consider to be the number one social strategy, it's important to note that both people in a relationship need to agree to use it for it to work. It's also important to remember that strategies are belief driven. They are not driven by habit, rote, prompting, or reminding. If you don't have the beliefs, you won't understand the strategies and you certainly won't use them.

The most important social strategy

The number one strategy everybody needs to know on or off the spectrum to be an effective communicator is the fine art of clarification. In my experience, that is it. Every communication strategy you will ever use is rooted in clarification. Now you may be thinking, "I knew that. That's simple and is common sense." Well, guess what? Hardly anybody does it. The people I have met, and I have met thousands, understand clarification as a concept, but they haven't taken the time to define it in a functional way and they never learned it as a concrete, deliberate strategy.

If you say that you clarify all the time, well, maybe you clarify some of the time, but I can almost guarantee that you do not clarify as often as you need to. For instance, have you ever experienced misunderstandings, arguments, or misperceptions in your relationships? How often after a misunderstanding do you say to yourself, "Oh well, next time I'll remember to ask or check in with you," and then you don't? This is because you haven't learned to believe clarification is critical, a priority, or essential. That is why you don't do it. In my life, I miss so much nonverbal information but I clarify that I have enough information to know what the heck is going on, and by doing so, my life has become so much easier.

Let's define *clarification* so we understand it in the same way. *Clarification* is checking in with the person you are communicating with in order to verify the message you received is the message the other person intended. The reverse is true as well.

One problem

Of course you remember to do that some of the time. What I am suggesting is that you need to do it as a habit and not on occasion. There is one obvious problem with this strategy, and it's that people generally resist clarifying. They resist checking in with each other. Has this been your experience? When you have attempted to clarify, have you received responses such as, "You should have been paying attention," or, "You should have listened the first time." If you have ever responded this way then understand that what you've done is criticize someone for clarifying with you. Do parents ever do this to their children or teachers with their students? Have you ever heard, "I don't like repeating myself"?

When someone gives you an opportunity to be better understood by clarifying and you become defensive, what happens? What do they learn about clarifying? They learn not to do it, and that it is dangerous because it makes you mad.

Because clarification is so critical to communication, I made a point of asking neurotypicals and spectrumites alike why they resist clarifying, and here's what I learned. The first reason is that people are generally overconfident in their own perception. They think they got it right the first time. Those people still have a lot of miscommunication and misunderstandings because they do not question their own perception. Even though they are proven incorrect time and time again, it doesn't occur to them to do anything different. Even worse is when they blame the other person for the miscommunication. There is even a word that describes the habit of thinking that you've got it right, don't need to clarify, and believe you have enough information without it. The word is *assumption*.

I know what you're thinking

People rely more on assumption than clarification even though it is incredibly unreliable. It is unreliable because assumption requires mind reading; it is guessing. There is no information gathering in assumption. Assumption is the false belief that communication has taken place without any proof. This is dangerous in a relationship and yet we all do it. I have done it myself and I am working diligently to do it less and less. People assume that they know what the other person meant, how the other person feels, and worst of all, they believe they know what the other person is thinking. Assuming you know what is going on in someone's internal life is the most absurd assumption. There are classes that talk about perspective taking and the importance of knowing what another person might be thinking. That's nonsense—learn to diplomatically ask what another person is thinking. Don't read a person's mind; ask him a question and clarify. Assumption causes communication problems and never solves them.

Have you ever assumed things while communicating, and if so, what were the results of having done so? Has it ever gone well? Sure, you might get it right on occasion. You might be working with somebody that you know very well, who is very predictable and relatively easy to read. Being able to read some people so well lulls you into a false sense of security.

Now think about the other person who assumes you understood him and, when there's a misunderstanding, blames you as though understanding was solely your responsibility. The problem was in the assumption and the fact that the clarification did not take place. Wouldn't it make more sense to clarify and make sure you understood him, or for him to make sure he was understood by you? Ask the questions, get the clarification, and you will not have to worry about it.

The problem with nonverbal communication

I've repeatedly read a statistic that states that nonverbal communication accounts for well over eighty-five percent of communication. If that is correct, we are all in big trouble, and the reason why that is, is because that means we are not talking to each other. We instead rely on hints, innuendos and suggestions so we don't have to talk to each other. I don't believe that over eighty-five percent of communication must be nonverbal; I believe it's our bodies communicating what we're afraid to talk about or don't know how to talk about. It isn't that we can't make a greater percentage of our communication verbal; it's that we don't. Why do we do this?

Again, how reliable is nonverbal communication in the first place? We all need to learn and remember that nonverbal communication is unreliable. It does not tell you what a person is thinking. It may give you some hints as to what a person is feeling but it does not tell you for certain. With my spectrum brain, nonverbal communication looks like a little dance people do in addition to their words that doesn't mean very much. So if there's more I need to know, I'd better ask, "Is there more I need to know that you haven't told me?" That invites the person to tell me if he wants me to know it. Though I could easily assume he's told me everything, walk away, have a misunderstanding, and blame him for not being clear enough in the first place.

What are you afraid of?

So, overestimating our own perception and assuming is one reason people don't clarify. But there is a bigger reason why people do not clarify, and what I have learned from talking to neurotypicals and spectrumites, and reflecting on my own experience, is they do not clarify because they are afraid the other person will be angry with them. Does that sound right to you? Are you afraid of asking the wrong questions, sounding too pushy, sounding rude, and not wanting somebody to be angry with you? So much in fact that you will risk miscommunication and misunderstanding just to avoid anger? The reality is that all you really accomplish by not clarifying at the time is postponing anger. You can ask now and maybe the other person will get upset with you, or you can walk away trusting your perception only to find out later you misunderstood and find she is angry with you because you misunderstood. Does that make sense?

You may think doing things this way makes people look pretty stupid. I wouldn't say stupid, I'd say unaware. People aren't paying attention to how they communicate, what's working and what isn't. What's worse is that the one strategy, clarification, is something we're taught from childhood to avoid doing. We learned the worst thing we could do is make someone else angry, and as a parent, I admit, I was guilty of this, too, at one point. Your children do things to push your buttons and you react by saying, "Don't make me angry!" It is the ultimate warning. What happens is we are teaching our children that our anger is their responsibility. So, it is their responsibility to not make us angry, even if it's at the expense of clarifying. Spend time thinking about that.

Stop punishing honesty

Another thing that interferes with clarification is a common difference between neurotypicals and spectrumites when it comes to communication. You may be familiar with the neurotypical tendency to prioritize feelings over facts. Would you say that is accurate? This is where the anger issue comes into it: "I want you to feel good. I want you to be happy with me, so I will tell you what I need to tell you so you feel good because I don't want you to be angry." Do you realize that lying is all about avoiding or delaying anger? People cover the truth, they offer compliments and they do it to help protect the other person and themselves from anger. In other words, feeling good is at the expense of effective communication. It doesn't make sense to communicate that way, especially to the spectrum mind. Why wouldn't you just be honest and tell the truth? Why wouldn't you use facts?

I have also experienced that anger can turn an honest spectrumite into a liar. You hear the stereotype—people on the spectrum don't lie. Well, guess what? If you are honest, you tend to be honest until you are yelled at and criticized often enough for being honest, that you learn to expect anger in response to honesty and you begin to protect yourself. So, a lot of these kids who are lying and deceiving, when I explore with them the reasons for it, say, "Well, my mom yells at me," or "I get in trouble." So the child learns that honesty brings pain and anger. It does not bring support. So, if you do not want your child to lie, don't give him a reason to. Don't punish honesty with anger and make it dangerous.

My eldest son is one of the most truthful people on the planet. He could not keep a secret to save his life. My middle son who is more challenged has received so much criticism that he began lying about everything. It was so extreme that if you asked him if he wanted a particular food, he'd say yes even though he didn't want it because he thought it would make us happy. Then when he was given the food, he wouldn't eat it, which caused more problems.

When I figured out what was going on with him, I began working on my own responses as well as helping him understand his own needs, and showing more obvious respect for them. It's becoming far easier for him to be truthful because I helped him understand that if he is honest with me, he will get support and understanding instead of anger.

Here's our predicament: What do you do when you value clarification but the person you want to clarify with gets angry or defensive? How do you talk to this person? Any thoughts?

An important agreement

You could simply stop talking to him or lie more but that won't change anything. Instead, let me teach you the key to solving the problem of how to bring clarification into your communication and getting rid of the habit of reacting with anger. You negotiate clarification. You explain the need for it, the problems it solves and agree to clarify with each other in order to increase understanding in your relationship.

A mother asked me how to clarify nonverbal cues. She pointed out that nonverbal cues can be misinterpreted in a negative way and people can become upset about it. I asked her to remember that nonverbal cues are not reliable. If you become angry it's because of an assumption that you knew what the cue meant. The solution is to check in with the person and see if what they did meant something. You'd clarify in this way: "I noticed you did [whatever it was] after I said [whatever you said], and I'm not sure how you took it. So could you tell me what you think I meant?"

This same mother explained that neurotypical people are taught to hide nonverbal behaviors that are easier to read in children who haven't learned to hide them yet. She said, "You can watch your children and know when they are happy or sad and when they are excited. Then you have children with ADHD or something like that, and they are very animated and you can really always tell how they are feeling, but then as we become adults, we lose a lot of that authenticity. So as adults, it is very hard to read a person's cues if he's good at masking."

I responded to her statement by saying, "Something you just said is very interesting. You watch what your children are doing and you know how they are feeling. This is an assumption. You may have some indications as to how they might feel but the only way you know what their experience is, is to check in with something like, 'It looks like you are happy. Is that correct?' Because some people have nervous laughter when they're uncomfortable, and if a child thinks laughter means happy and he is doing something that makes the parent laugh nervously, he will do it more, thinking the parent enjoys it."

Now here's where it gets really confusing for the child: The laughing parent suddenly gets angry and tells the child to stop it. Now the child wonders why you were happy one second and angry the next. The fact is you weren't happy but the child didn't know that. The nervous laughter needed to be explained to him as nervousness, along with what's causing the nervousness, and what he can do about it. The fact is, what appears to be happiness can be anxiety and what appears as anger can actually be fear. Don't assume it; clarify it.

In order to be able to make clarification a priority in your relationships, you need to have a belief about clarification that makes it a priority. By *belief*, I don't mean simply thinking that clarification is a good idea. A belief is something you feel, and when you don't do what you believe, you feel extremely uncomfortable. If it's simply a good idea, you may forget it and not notice. But when you go against a belief, you know it. Understand?

Ask, ask, ask

The belief that reinforces valuing clarification is, "I must be certain I know what a person is thinking or feeling, and the only way to be certain is by asking." Certainty isn't achievable with assumption. When you must be certain, and you trust nothing else but asking, you will be compelled to ask. You understand that your perception is imperfect and that the only way you will know is to clarify.

With this belief, when you see someone who seems happy, you'll realize she might be happy but you don't know and won't be sure until you clarify. So, you have a belief that says, "I don't have enough information until I ask." If I haven't asked, I don't know. I'm guessing and some people unfortunately mistake guessing and assumptions for knowledge. That is where misunderstanding occurs.

Do you always have to ask how a person is feeling or thinking? The answer is you don't always have to ask, but remember that if you choose not to, what you perceive is an assumption and not fact until you clarify. Don't make the mistake of deciding something without the clarification that gives you enough information to decide. All right?

Clarify for the literal mind

Here's an interesting problem. How do you teach the value of clarification to the spectrumite who takes everything literally? Who insists she heard it right even when others try and explain themselves. This is the curse of immaculate perception that we discussed earlier, the belief that your perception is spotless. The default setting of the spectrum mind is to take things literally which is all the more reason for us to clarify. I tend to take things literally at first. Being aware of this, I've also learned that if something that was said upsets me, the first thing I must do is clarify. When I do, I give the person a chance to say it differently. I then hear it differently, and my feelings change for the better.

What if the literal thinker doesn't have the awareness of her literal thinking? She thinks she's right and knows exactly what you meant and what you're thinking. Due to her extreme subjectivity, she may think her thoughts are everyone else's thoughts, too. So if she thinks it, you must be thinking it, too. Here's how you can introduce clarification into your relationship with her: "I heard you say that you think you know what I'm thinking. Well, the fact is I don't know what you're thinking. When I say something to you, I don't know how you're going to respond so I don't always choose the perfect words. I choose the words I can think of, then I need you to tell me what you think I meant so I can give you more words to explain what I really meant until I've used enough words for us to understand each other."

Now I know that sounds complex, but think more about the spirit of the statement. You want to explain to her that mind reading isn't a skill of yours, and it takes a few times to get all of the words out that help you best get your point across. Does that help? I still have a literal mind, but with increased self-awareness, I've learned to take the way my mind works into account when communicating. I clarify to determine whether something is meant literally or as an expression. Those I've negotiated to clarify with are used to this and will tell me.

The object of social strategies must not be to teach us to make our minds do things they don't do. It's unreasonable and disrespectful. We need the awareness of how our minds work in a social situation, what information we perceive and what we miss. Then help us learn how to get that information through clarifying, instead of reading unreliable nonverbal cues. Meet us halfway.

We all want to be understood, but we must be flexible in how we get the information we need from each other. We need to emphasize the product over the process. I've become who I am today through negotiating my relationships in terms of what we need from each other, not from making myself into someone I'm not to make the other person happy at my expense.

What's the protocol?

I'm living proof, as are my clients, that this is achievable, teachable, and best of all, it is generalizable. Regardless of what is appropriate and what other people are used to, clarification can work with anybody in any situation, even when you don't know the rules of a situation. There are different people, different scenarios, and different protocols, and you can clarify by asking, "Excuse me, how is this supposed to go?" "What is my role here?" "What would you like me to do?" That is a very innocent way of clarifying to find out what the social protocol is instead of saying, "I have bad social skills and I don't know what to do here." You say, "Excuse me, I'm new here and I have not done this before. What is my role? What would you like me to do?" That is a perfect way for spectrumites to ask for the information they need without disclosing they're on the spectrum.

Keep in mind; I have spent upwards of twenty years thinking this through, so this makes much more sense in my head. I devote my time to figuring out how to make communication more effective without it being a source of pain for me or the other person.

I don't get it

There are spectrumites who give up on learning how to make communication work. Instead, they make excuses. They'll isolate themselves, play video games all day and refuse to talk to other people and justify it by saying, "I have autism. I don't get that social stuff." It's also fair to say that they don't know what they don't know; they just know that socializing is confusing. As I mentioned earlier, spectrumites need to learn what the nonverbal frequency is communicating and how to get that information another way. They may not even know nonverbal communication exists and may be relying on the incomplete verbal feedback they get. Then after years of misunderstandings and hurt feelings they may finally get sick of it and simply quit trying.

If you don't know about it, you certainly don't have the option to ask for it. The first step in helping the spectrumite who has reached this point is to ask him to share what other people say and do that he finds confusing. Start the conversation there to move his awareness from "nothing works" to "exactly what isn't working." Once you know what the problem is, you can define it, and find a strategy to solve it.

Problem solved

How do you know when you've clarified enough? When you've clarified that both of you understand what action you are going to take based on the conversation. You'd say, "Based on what you said, I'm hearing that you want me to do this in this way. Is that correct?" When the other person confirms your understanding of the action you'll take, then you have complete clarification.

What's the best way to teach clarification to a young child? By modeling it—don't just explain it; do it when communicating with him. Ask questions and tell him why you are doing it the way you are doing it. Example: "I am clarifying so that I can understand you better. I want to show you the respect of making sure I understand you as much as possible. I want you to understand me as much as possible too so we can feel good about talking with each other."

Explain the reason for clarifying and the critical piece, the problems being solved by doing so. The social skills approach is: "You say hi to someone when he says hi because it's polite." That's rote. It doesn't teach you what problem is solved by doing that or what need is being met. It's mechanical without meaning or a belief behind it.

What problems does being appropriate solve? Appropriateness solves the problem of people criticizing you because you were not appropriate. What problem does it solve for you in terms of communication, in terms of connecting with the other person? That goes undefined. But if you are modeling clarification, you get to explain why you clarify. "I can't read minds, so it would be disrespectful for me to think that I know what you are thinking or what you are feeling and that is why I am asking."

There are some people who seem to expect mind reading and say, "Well, you should know me well enough by now. You should just know." When you clarify, you emphasize that you know her well enough to care about and respect her, which is why you are not going to show her the disrespect of thinking you know her so well that you can afford not to ask her for clarification. It is part of what brings us closer.

A father asked me how to teach his son to clarify when others are bored with him. I miss boredom a lot when talking to people, so this is how I ask for clarification. I say, "I've talked a lot about this. Would you like to hear more or would you like to change the subject?" That is how I get clarification as to whether a person is bored, and it give others the opportunity to alleviate that boredom by verbalizing what they may have been communicating nonverbally.

I also remind myself to give people a chance to talk instead of monologuing. I ask, "Did you want to respond to that?" or "Do you have an opinion about that?" Because I know if someone is making a gesture or two to let me know that she wants to chime in, I won't always catch it and I need to ask. That is why clarification is so important. If I don't ask, I won't know.

Chapter 10

The Art of Negotiation

All relationships are negotiated. The quality of the relationships you are currently in is exactly what you have agreed to, whether you realize it or not. We'll discuss how negotiations are made with particular focus on negotiating the relationship you want to have with your child.

The ideal negotiations result in two people being able to work together using their complementary skills to better each other's lives through their collaboration. A perfect example of this is my relationship with my wife Cathy. We are complementary in such ideal ways that when we work together strategically the results we get are amazing. I am extremely auditory, and Cathy is very visual. She is far better at picking up the nonverbal information but misses a lot of what is said. I pick up a lot of what is said and I miss the stuff that she sees. Together we can collaborate to complement each other's understanding of a situation in order to get a clearer picture. When we're on the same page, we make a joint decision about how to proceed. That is the epitome of partnership.

Having such complementary skill-sets has its advantages, but it can also lead to misunderstandings because we filter information so differently. We really had to work hard to figure out where the disconnects were in our communication, and at the beginning of our relationship, there were many really heated arguments because of these disconnects. We finally realized that we needed to take some time and figure out what was missing and how to fill in the gaps in our understanding to stop these arguments. Eventually we figured out a way to communicate with each other in a respectful, reciprocal way that allows us to be more effective as a couple and as parents. We are adamant about modeling our communication strategies to our three sons who are very different from each other and have experienced the same frequency of misunderstandings that Cathy and I had. Where they used to fight more often than not, they are now more effective at clarifying and self-advocating with each other. The result is they enjoy each other's company on a daily basis. If we can do it, you can do it.

What do you believe?

As with our conversation about clarification, your ability to effectively negotiate your relationships depends upon the beliefs you have. Your beliefs about how relationships work, your role and responsibilities in them, what you say, and what you do all have beliefs that justify them. The reason you shake hands when you meet someone is because you believe that is something important to do. The reason you make eye contact is because you believe it is important to make eye contact. People on the spectrum do what they do because their beliefs tell them it is important for them to do things the way they do them.

Let's begin discussing negotiation by defining it. How do you define *negotiation*? Some have described it as establishing give-and-take or common ground. Negotiation establishes agreements about the responsibilities of each person in the relationship. Some believe negotiation is about agreeing what you're willing to give up to get what you want.

Take a moment to reflect upon your definition of negotiation, as it will shed light on your beliefs about it. Now let me offer you the first belief you must have before negotiation can even take place. The belief that "All relationships are negotiated." That means that people in relationships negotiate or agree on, either verbally or nonverbally, how to relate to each other. A negotiation in a relationship is an agreement about how to do "us." It is an agreement of the "dos" and "don'ts" of that relationship. Does that definition make sense to you?

The role of being right

I want you to think about this. It is a bit of a rhetorical question. Have you thought of negotiation as taking the necessary time to convince the other person how right you are? Or have you known someone who thinks of negotiation like that? I have met so many people like this, spectrum and neurotypical alike. They think that they have the most informed position on the matter and negotiation consists of being willing to hear them out so they can convince you of how wrong you are and how right they are. In fact, if you think your job in a conversation is to wear somebody down into submission until he agrees, that is not negotiation—it's more like bullying.

When I point this out to people on the spectrum who do it, especially those who feel themselves on the receiving end of bullying, they are shocked to hear that comparison because they don't realize that is what they are doing—being so disrespectful to another person's point of view and another person's right to be heard and offer his contribution to a conversation. That is an important point to understand. It is only negotiation when the opinions and needs of both parties involved are respected and their needs are met as close to win–win as possible. If a person believes that relationships are based on win–lose, right or wrong, strength versus weakness, then they are competitive, not cooperative. Do you feel that your relationship with the spectrumite in your life is competitive and feels like an argument too much of the time?

If you'd like that to change, you need to start with your beliefs about your role as a parent. Many of us are raised to believe that the parent–child relationship is win–lose. Parents have all the power and all the say. When you have a child on the spectrum, this belief tends to get pushed into overdrive because your child can be so resistant to you that you are compelled to dig in and impose your will with greater intensity. Sound familiar?

In order to begin shifting your relationship toward a more win–win agreement, it is important that you begin to understand that the "because I said so" way of parenting is out if you are going to model negotiation and agreement. The "my way or the highway" approach is history because it is destructive in that it is based on power instead of collaboration. I know that this is a hard shift to make because I have not told you yet how to begin making that shift. I am addressing the beliefs first because if the beliefs aren't in place, the strategies won't be anything you'll see as useful and you certainly won't be compelled to apply them if you don't believe in them.

There is one exception to negotiation and that is in matters of safety. Our two youngest sons had the dangerous habit of running into the street without looking for cars first. Now, in that instance we are going to yell "STOP!" at the top of our lungs. If your child is playing with something sharp or dangerous, you need to step in and say stop for matters of safety. Negotiation comes in later when you touch base with the child and explain why you handled the situation that way. You explain the safety issue from the standpoint that one of your agreements as a parent is to keep them safe, and this will allow you to restore that sense of collaboration and respect again.

Nonverbal communication doesn't help

In the neurotypical world you can observe a person's nonverbal reactions to what you say and do; you can then adjust how you relate to that person accordingly. This adjustment is an example of an unspoken negotiation. You don't even know you are doing it. You just automatically watch the feedback and adjust so you end up doing what the other person likes and avoid doing what the other person doesn't like. Hopefully she is paying attention to you and getting the same kind of feedback and making the same kind of adjustments. You nonverbally negotiate what to do and not to do with each other, but in the spectrum world, as you know, the nonverbal is the very information we miss. If we miss that feedback, then we certainly can't use it to make the necessary adjustments.

When you are negotiating with a spectrumite, it needs to be communicated in a more verbal and concrete way. And if not verbal, then written. I have many friends on the spectrum that I communicate with through various forms of social media and e-mail because they are more comfortable with that medium than the overwhelming experience of a face-to-face conversation. It is written, more concrete, much more succinct, and easier to get their feedback than to try and decode all of the abstract, unreliable nonverbal information.

Rules of engagement

There are three main things that you negotiate in relationships:

1. You are going to give each other feedback on what is not working in your partnership. In my case, I know that I miss a lot of the visual cues. I also know I can ramble on and on if I get really excited about a topic—and I know that can sometimes be overwhelming for somebody, so I want feedback when I am doing that and do not notice it. In my relationship with Cathy, for instance, I will ask her

for feedback on that specific tendency—when I am talking too much, I would like to know that she would like a turn or has spotted that somebody else would like a turn talking and I haven't noticed it.

2. You will determine exactly how to give each other feedback. I want feedback but I want it in such a way that I don't feel like I was just punched in the gut. It is easier to hear feedback and use it when it is supportive instead of critical. Therefore, I negotiate how I can be given that feedback. I can negotiate an obvious hand signal that Cathy and I have agreed to. I can negotiate her saying something very gentle to me such as, "Excuse me, I would like to add something here." That is how she lets me know, and because we negotiated that phrase, I know that phrase means specifically this: "Hey, Brian, you have been talking too long, you need to pause and let someone else contribute." The spoken word is critical here in relating to me because I am so auditory. I had a client with a tendency to get louder as he talked, so we negotiated between him and his siblings that they would use a hand signal to cue him to lower his voice. The signal was subtle and allowed him to get the feedback he needed to adjust without feeling like he has been outed or criticized in front of everybody in the room. That is why it is important to negotiate both what to give feedback on and specifically how to give it.

3. You agree to how you will receive the feedback. This is a very important point. Some people will say, "Be honest with me," and when you are, they get mad. Why would you want to give feedback to a person who will only get angry with you? Negotiating this third step is where you solve that problem.

In Step 1, you negotiate precisely what you want to receive feedback on. In Step 2, you determine how to give feedback so you know it when you're getting it, in the way you're able to accept it. After negotiating all that, why would you get angry? If a person is giving you what you asked for in the way you asked for it, there is no reason to be angry. Instead, you negotiate to receive the feedback with gratitude, not anger. Then the first time a person does give you feedback in the agreed-upon way, and you do respond the way you agreed to, guess what you are going to get? Trust, because you kept your end of the agreement. Then you'll get more feedback, more clarification, and more opportunities to improve your relationship.

Can you repeat that?

Negotiating to clarify, as I mentioned earlier, is critical. Parents and teachers alike sometimes insist that children ask for help, but then when they do, say, "You're supposed to pay attention," "I don't want to repeat myself," or "Weren't you listening?" That is hypocrisy at its finest. It amazes me how often I've encountered adults who treat a request to repeat something as an insult when all the child wants is to make sure she got it right. With my own son, I will ask if he heard what I said. When he says he did, I ask him to repeat it. Quite often he apologizes because he, in fact, wasn't paying attention. But jumping on him, shaming him and saying he should be paying attention is not the solution. The point here is that he was honest. He tuned out for a second, and who doesn't? You can't pay attention one hundred percent of the time, especially if you are on the spectrum. Paying attention is hard and we frequently check out.

What I teach my sons and my clients is that if they do not hear something, they should just ask me to repeat it, because I know then that it is important enough to them that they want me to repeat it. They are doing me the courtesy of letting me know they want to hear what I said and I respect that by repeating it. If your child's teachers are not understanding this basic rule, you have to explain to them that she is trying to learn in their class, and the more they criticize her for asking questions, the more they teach her that asking questions is a punishable offense, which will negatively impact her education. It flies right in the face of what teachers are trying to accomplish so they need to be called on it.

Ask teachers what their beliefs are about your child's role in the classroom. Is the belief that your child needs to be giving the teacher his undivided attention the entire time? If that is correct, my question to the teacher is, "Do you do that? In any situation in your life, have you tuned out or thought about something else, lost focus?" They would be lying to you if they said that never happened. It is part of the human experience. So, if they admit it themselves, that they tune out, and of course, need to ask whomever they were talking to to repeat the question, then maybe they need to extend our kids the same respect. That has got to happen. As parents, we need to remember it and practice it or we have no credibility when encouraging the teacher to do it.

Don't touch me

One component of communication that is tricky to negotiate but still requires special consideration is the role of touch. Shaking hands, tapping, or touching someone on the arm or leg during conversation is common for many people to do. For those with touch sensitivity, however, this repeated touching could be a source of great stress.

If somebody touches me lightly and does it repeatedly, my skin crawls unless I rub that spot. It's as though the touch creates an intense itch that must be scratched. There have been a few occasions when I have had to tell someone I am sensitive to touch and that it is distracting me from hearing her, explaining that for me to hear and for her to be heard, touching needs to be avoided. This is an example of negotiating how to do "us." It is a request meant to help our relationship as opposed to a criticism of her.

However, if someone asks you for a tap on the shoulder or knee to let her know she's talking too loud, then touch helps the relationship. The issue I described with my sensitivity is too much touch.

It's all about "We"

Another critical element for effective negotiation to take place is the understanding that every relationship has three components: You, Me, and We. It's an agreement about how to do "We," after all. So it's important to realize and value the fact that whereas each person has a set of needs, the relationship itself has needs, too. Needs to maintain the connection between both you and me.

Of course, this can be particularly challenging when you're relating to a spectrumite that has the "It's all about me" mind-set. I had that very same mind-set for decades. I believed I was the absolute center of the universe: "The world happened to me," "I am a big victim," "God hates me." Cathy and I have to deal with that all of the time, especially with our eldest son and his "Give me, give me, give me, I want more, more, more, more, I want, I want, I want." We have to remind him about You, Me, and We constantly. That relationships aren't about one person using everyone else to get his needs met.

I've spent years researching and asking questions about relationships in order to help myself become more effective at creating and maintaining the relationships I want and need to be in. I find it fascinating what people have decided to believe about relationships even when these beliefs cause them problems.

Some people believe that the priority is to make sure their own needs are met in relationships, while others think their responsibility is to make sure that the other person is happy. They see it as an either–or proposition. Is there a problem with that kind of thinking? The problem is that one person always suffers. One person always has to settle for less. When relating to spectrumites, is there often a tendency for them to prioritize one person's needs over another's? Their own, unfortunately. However, give enough criticism to a spectrumite for being selfish, and the tendency can be to swing to the other extreme in which they learn that their responsibility is to make other people happy. I've worked with numerous clients who have been on the receiving end of behavior modification therapies. Without exception, they report that the biggest lesson those methods teach them is that their needs don't matter and that they only succeed when the person keeping score is happy.

These behavior methods result in a swing from selfish to selfless to a destructive degree. Why, oh, why doesn't anyone teach them balance? Because such behavioral approaches are win–lose, that's why. They're about compliance, obedience, and not about the partnership that fulfilling relationships are based on.

The problem solver

I realize that a relationship with someone on the spectrum is likely to begin as win–lose by default until you negotiate otherwise. We'll discuss exactly how to begin doing that. And yes, raising children on the spectrum is exhausting; I'm raising three of them. If you're beginning the negotiation after years of agreeing to be your child's designated problem solver, rescuer, and advocate, then it can be a real kicking and screaming match at the start. Asking a child to move from being enabled to empowered is a scary proposition for them.

Every day we are met with children who become bored at some point and want to be entertained. If there is a problem and Cathy or I don't drop everything we're doing to fix the problem, they get angry at her because it is her job to solve the problem. Have you had this experience?

The parents are the problem solvers and how dare they not do so upon command. That is win–lose and we need to change that. What's even worse are the parents of a spectrumite who realize they're doing most or all of the giving, ask themselves about their own needs, and then feel guilty about thinking of themselves. Sound familiar?

Reversing selfishness

If you make excuses for your child being so needy and you don't do things to require him to have a more balanced relationship with you, you are actually enabling him to remain helpless because you are allowing yourself to stay in the role of rescuer. For both of your sakes, that must shift.

Before I can tell you how to make this shift, I have to introduce a few terms to you. One I invented and it is nothing fantastic, but it is a word that really helps encapsulate this idea. *Selfish* refers to an emphasis on Me in the You, Me, and We relationship. It's Me at the expense of You and We. You see this with a child who bugs her brother because she's bored, or with an adult or child who thinks you're selfish because their needs don't come first. This is a win–lose situation.

Selfless is also win–lose because it focuses on the You at the expense of Me and We. Selfless people work very hard to solve the problem of how to please everybody and keep everybody happy. Wanting to make everybody happy is a form of perfectionism. We've all heard and even dispensed the advice that you can't please everyone. But few people have any idea how to internalize it and practice it.

Here is the new term. This is the term that emphasizes the We of the You, Me, and We—the partnership. The word is *selfus*. It is focused on the role that I play in supporting our partnership, so that we both benefit. It prioritizes the win–win.

Selfus is very conscious of the fact that doing my work for the partnership helps you do yours. It values reciprocity. You negotiate to reach agreement on how to do "We," and clarify to see how well you are doing at it. See how this all comes together? You start with clarification and making sure we are getting feedback as we need it, negotiating the things we are going to give feedback on, and the You, Me, and We are the things we negotiated to prioritize.

There are specific beliefs that bring You, Me, and We, clarification, and negotiation to life as active parts of your relationships instead of allowing them to be occasional events you have to remember to do. Your belief is that both people must benefit from the conversation you are having. In order to make sure you're acting from that belief, ask yourself this question before even talking to the other person: "What problems are being solved for You, Me, and We by the statement I am about to make or the question I am about to ask?"

If it is not going to benefit both people, then you need to think about whether it is worth even asking that question. If it is completely selfish, if it is going to cost her too much, it may solve a problem for you, but at her expense. If you are totally selfless, you are going to step in and give one more thing even though you've got nothing left, but you are doing yourself a disservice because you are volunteering to be on the losing end of a win–lose. Because you are not asking for anything in return, you're not asking for any help in balancing the give-and-take in the relationship.

A spectrumite who uses the criteria of "What problems are being solved by this statement or question?" is less likely to monologue about his special interests with no concern about how it impacts the other person. Why would you monologue endlessly if you were concerned the other person might not be interested? You wouldn't. Instead the likelier approach would be to ask if she wants to hear about it. Does that sound like clarification? If she is interested, then you also clarify to see when she has heard enough. Always thinking in terms of You, Me, and We. That if what we are talking about doesn't help the We, the partnership, then it's best either not to do it or to negotiate how to do it so that it works for the partnership.

Being a follower

Let's think more about how communication strategies can either cause or solve problems. I received an e-mail from a parent asking how to teach her son not to be a follower in social situations.

A follower is a child who does whatever he is told by a peer, sometimes to the point of doing things you feel he understands are the wrong things to do. A follower is in selfless mode. One of my sons is a follower. Why do you think children choose to follow?

Is it to fit in and be accepted? Is it because it takes less effort than being a leader? Is it because they trust the people they are following? Let's look a little deeper. For some people, if things simply move too fast for them to make a decision on what to do, it is much easier to defer to somebody else. Cathy has a large family that likes to get together at holidays and we've negotiated that I will follow her lead during holiday gatherings because it's too chaotic for me to focus most of the time.

Being in selfless mode, people pleasing, is also a way to avoid criticism. If you robotically follow the leader, you'll be praised for going along. One of the problems caused by leading is that you open yourself up to criticism; so following is always the safest thing to do. Remember this when advising your child to think for himself, it's an important value but one that comes with great risk for a child unprepared to endure the storm of criticism for doing so. It is important to have the discussion and ask: what problems would be caused for you if you took the lead? Until you solve those problems, it will be too dangerous to do anything other than follow. It is not as simple as asking a child to step up and take the lead.

Teaching "We"

If relationships require that the needs of both people be met in order to have a win–win, you start teaching this by acknowledging the win–lose. If you are experiencing someone operating from a win–lose perspective, call him on it. If you have a husband who ignores you when you ask for something and you want a conversation, you can say, "Excuse me, I just want to clarify something here. It seems like every time I need some information, you refuse to give it to me, and you get your way because you don't have to talk, but I lose because I don't get the information, and that doesn't work. This is a relationship where there are two of us, and I very much value our partnership but I recognize that we both have needs to be met for our relationship to work. One of my needs is for information, to know how I am doing, and so far you are deciding not to give me that information. So, our relationship is very win–lose right now and that doesn't work."

Also keep in mind that this partner no doubt is getting things from you that you are used to giving, have always given, and don't negotiate access to. Let me give you an example: Parents have a tendency to simply give to their children in a selfless way because it's our responsibility to give them what they need. But no one ever said our kids don't have to earn what they get. If a child is used to being given to, she can begin to feel entitled to those things because they have always been given without condition. In order for a child to understand the win–win, it is important that she realizes and experiences the give-and-take requirement of a reciprocal relationship.

It takes your energy and resources to give her things. Now don't say it in a way that makes her feel guilty for everything you do for her. That is not the point. You want to teach her gratitude. You are happy to give her something, but you want her to understand that it takes a tremendous amount of effort and expense to give it to her, so asking for something in return requires both people to work at the relationship so it can be more win–win.

Let me give you another example: My eldest son—who always wants more and expresses very little gratitude—came to me very excited about a new video game he had just learned about. I was in the middle of something for my business, but he wanted me to drop everything and take him right then and there and go buy it for him. I responded using clarification, negotiation, and You, Me, and We with him in the following way.

He said, "Dad, there's this great new game. It just came out and it's only thirty dollars, and the game store is just down the street.

It's not that far away so it won't take us that long. Can you take me there right now?"

In his mind it was all about him, and I was just supposed to take him down there and it was no big deal. This scenario may sound familiar to you. In the past, Cathy and I have responded to our kids' selfishness with our own selfishness, saying things like, "You're so selfish and all you think about is you and you never care about us." Of course, in that case, we're responding to win–lose with more win–lose in the form of blaming and criticism. What gets missed is helping him understand what will work, while we emphasize what isn't working.

Now that I know better, when my son came to me with this big request, I kept in mind my values of making sure that our needs were met, not just his. I want to strengthen our relationship and go for the win–win. The first thing I did was clarify my understanding of just what he was asking.

I said, "Let me see if I understand you correctly. It sounds as though you are asking me to stop what I am doing, and use my car and my gas in order to take you to spend my money on a game for you. Am I hearing you correctly?" Thus reflecting back to him that I heard him make a very one-sided request. Then his enthusiasm started to deflate a little bit.

He said, "Well, no. You could play it, too, I suppose."

I said, "So, you suppose I might be able to play a game that I bought? That maybe I could play it?" He said, "Sure."

I clarified with him further, "One of the issues is that I don't like to play video games so buying a video game that I won't play seems like it won't help me at all. Would it make sense for me to buy something I don't like? I understand the idea of how buying the game would be very exciting for you; you seem very excited about it." He said, "Yeah, it's a really cool game."

I said, "So, if you really want me to do this for you, it is very important that you help me, so doing this for you is much more of a fair deal so we both get something out of it."

I then clarified a value with him that I know is very important to the vast majority of us, especially spectrumites. I said, "You do like things when they are fair, don't you?"

He said, "Yes, I do like when things are fair."

I said, "Well, this is how we are going to make it fair." Notice how I introduced the word *we* at this point. I began by pointing out the win–lose disparity in his request, and then discussed how his needs and my needs required attention; next I explained how *we* would make it happen together. So I explained, "If you want this game and you want me to use my car, my gas, and my money, then it is only fair that I get something, too. You asked me to stop what I am doing and did not stop to ask me if what I was doing was important to me. One way to make this fair for me is if you wait until tomorrow to have me take you. That way I can finish what I am doing and you get to have your game."

Now, he got a little anxious because he had come to me in selfish mode, fully expecting to get the game now. I told him I understood that he wanted it right now, but if he wanted to get it, he needed my car, my gas, and my money. The only way I could give it to him was if I got what I needed as well. So, I said I would take the time to get him there and back tomorrow but that there were some things I needed him to do. First, I needed time to finish what I was doing and there was also some cleaning to be done around the house, and if I had to do that also, I wouldn't have time to take him. I suggested that if he wanted to do those things it would free up my time, and then when I was done with work, I would have the time to take him to get his game with my car, my gas, and my money.

And I threw in a bonus for me. I said that since this was an expensive game, we needed to agree on how long it would be before he could ask me to spend any money on him again for a game or toy. So, we negotiated the details and said if we could agree to all of this, then it would be fair to both of us. We would both get our needs met; he could have his game and I could get done what I needed to.

In the end, he ended up doing more cleaning than I asked for; he thanked me for taking the time to discuss the issue. Where in the past I would just say no, we can't afford it, you're selfish, don't come to me that way, this time I actually explained to him why his approach caused a problem for our relationship—it was not about "We," it was just about him. Instead of getting upset about it, I pointed out the win–lose. I know this sounds complicated and I spend months training people on how to understand and apply these strategies because it requires shifting your beliefs and values to win–win thinking, and that is the toughest work. When you believe in win–win, you'll catch it when you aren't getting it as opposed to simply trying to remember the principle.

So when you're dealing with a selfish child or a selfish spouse, you need to internalize, embody, and model the value of *selfus*. Until that shift happens for you, you won't be able to convincingly say to the person that there is a partnership between you that needs to be strengthened and begin to negotiate the means for strengthening it. If you have a husband who is hiding and you are doing a thousand things, guess who controls the resources in the house? You have a lot more to negotiate than you are leveraging. You can renegotiate the things you've been providing for free and begin asking for payment in the form of communication. Of course, there is going to be pushback because you have been doing it this way for a long time. You have been letting him get away with the win–lose so there will be some resistance, and it may take a lot of support to get you through that rough period, but it is doable and necessary; otherwise things are going to continue as they are. This is how you use clarification, negotiation, and You, Me, and We together.

Everyday leverage

How do you apply this to a five-year-old or anyone else with a short attention span? A father shared the following scenario with me. His wife has a business in the house, and their son is always playing around, making a mess, and they repeatedly tell him not to play with Mommy's things.

The feedback their son was getting was, "Stop it." That kind of feedback is about the parents needs; it's only telling him to stop what they don't like. I encouraged the father to negotiate You, Me and We by saying, "When you do these things, although it might be fun for you, it [describe the problem it causes me] when you do that, and if you do things that cause me this problem, then I cannot do this for you." You decide what the "this" is. He needs to understand how this causes you a problem, and if he wants to play with things you don't want him to, then it's only fair if you get to play with his toys and not stop playing with them when he asks. He needs to know that what he does affects the relationship, and the rules he wants to follow are the ones you get to follow, too, in relating to him.

This father shared that they use going to the library and checking out books as a reward for good behavior, but that it was starting to lose its effectiveness. I emphasized the importance of using everyday things for leverage, not special bonuses. The things that he comes to you for that only you can provide.

There's a great example of this from my own life. There was an occasion with our eldest son in which he let Cathy know that he was out of clean underwear. She said, "I am very sorry that I didn't have time to do the laundry while shopping for the groceries to feed you. Since I did that for you, if you would like to have clean underwear today, I suggest you do a load of laundry." What do you think he ended up doing? The laundry.

We use this approach with each of our sons, including the five-year-old. We will watch him, of course, for safety reasons. In our family, we share responsibility for creating the problem of dirty laundry, and we all play a role in solving it. Therefore, in the case of the father whose son won't leave Mommy's things alone, turn the things he's used to simply getting into things he must participate in, or he doesn't get the benefit of it. If our five-year-old can do this, so can yours.

Keeping your agreements

In the scenario where I negotiated the purchase of a video game in exchange for time and chores, the outcome was achieved relatively problem free. There are other times when he will ask continuously—even if he ended up cleaning the house, the next day he would want something else, forgetting he agreed not to ask for something else for a month.

When this happens I remind him of our agreement and that if he continues asking for something he will be breaking the deal and therefore losing what I had agreed to get him.

When doing this with your child make sure that the loss of [whatever it is] was clearly explained in the very beginning as a consequence of breaking the deal. Otherwise it will seem like it came out of nowhere and he'll probably become very upset. When you establish this during the negotiation, make sure he says it back to you specifically and agrees to it: "I agree to not ask you to buy me any other toy for a month." Then you need to agree on what the consequence is if he breaks the deal, especially after you follow through. Example: "If you break the deal, we are going to take it back to the store." Have him verbally agree to that, too, and be very clear that you fully intend on following through. You must be prepared to do it and explain while doing it that your agreements with him are very important to you and you want him to trust you, and if you didn't keep your end of the deal, it would make you a liar and you're not going to lie to him. You made an agreement and you're sticking to it. Because in our relationship we need to be able to trust each other and we need to know that when we make an agreement, we'll keep it. See how that explanation had You, Me, and We in it? It describes the three components of your relationship and how they each depend on each other for your relationship to work.

One more example is an agreement Cathy made with our eldest son in response to a very rough week in which he seemed to be criticizing his brothers for everything they did. He wanted a new set of headphones for his cell phone and he wanted forty dollars to buy them and he wanted them right away. He originally offered to clean his bedroom and the basement. Cathy told him she didn't think that really benefited her in any way since it was a mess that he created and that he should be cleaning up after himself anyhow. Then he said he would cook dinner. She asked if he was going to eat dinner and he said yes. Cathy pointed out that as a member of the household he needed to be part of the dinner process anyway so that didn't benefit her. Then he spent about an hour trying to come up with something that would benefit Cathy and his agreement was that he would not fight with his brothers for a week.

She proposed that he go for a week without criticizing his brothers, and instead of bossing them around and bullying them, he would compliment them more and be patient with them. He thought about it and he decided that he was going to give it a try. The three of us agreed that if he made it the entire week, Cathy would take him to the store and give him the money for the headphones. However, if he did not keep the agreement and at some point during the week he criticized one of his brothers, the deal was off and he was not allowed to ask for anything else for one month.

We had him repeat what the agreement was to clarify that we were agreeing to the same thing. He was able to go the entire week without criticizing his brothers. There were a few evenings where he walked around mumbling to himself or went up to his room and spent some time alone when he found himself getting frustrated, but he went the entire week without criticizing. When the time came to honor our agreement, I handed him the money, and though he was very excited about getting the headphones, he said that, more than anything, he was proud of himself for the fact that he was able to change the way he spoke to his brothers.

During that week we didn't allow him to suffer in silence, we knew how hard it was for him. We made sure we supported him in this agreement by letting him know how well he was doing to help keep his spirits and motivation up. When he was mumbling to himself and the times he told us it was really hard because they were making him mad, we would point out to him that in the past he would have yelled at them, but now he wasn't, and he was also keeping the agreement he made to us and himself which is a sign of self respect as he was keeping his word.

We were amazed that he did it because of the amount of self-control it took. The negotiation and the supportive feedback helped him make it possible. Keep in mind that negotiation is something we've been using with our children for quite some time which is why these examples have such wonderful results. We experienced the same resistance in the beginning that you will. Keep it up and make it a part of your everyday life to really build them up. Remember, our relationships are built on agreements of how to do "us." The more common agreements are made, the better understood the boundaries in your relationships and the needs of the relationship will be. Absolutely no mind reading; discuss it, clarify, and negotiate.

The Three Gs

There is one more strategy to help spectrumites learn the give-and-take of a win–win relationship. The belief that informs this strategy is that information gets communicated in only two ways: by either making statements or asking questions. The purpose of making a statement is to deliver information. The purpose of a question is to gather information. Now before you know what statement to make or what question to ask, you need to know the goal that will be accomplished by doing so.

The strategy that will enable you to accomplish this is the Three Gs. This is the strategy that I use that allows me to make sure that my conversations are reciprocal, back and forth, and it also reminds me to listen to the other person. This strategy has only three steps, and is very simple and effective:

1. Goal

2. Give

3. Get.

The *goal* is the reason you are having the conversation. What do you want to get out of it? What information do you need to *give* the other person to let him know what your goal is, and what information do you hope to *get* by asking questions in order to accomplish your goal? That's it. Before I talk to anybody, I run through these three steps in my head so I'm ready to have the conversation with them.

I just have to note here that this is why chitchat is so difficult for us—there is no point to it, no goal; it seems to be talking simply to talk. If there is no goal to it, we don't know where it's headed, when it will end, and at some point we'll get exhausted because we have paid attention too long. Some of us simply get up and leave without saying anything and are accused of being rude, when in actuality we don't know how else to end the conversation. So please, when speaking to us, have a clear purpose and state that purpose so we'll know how long we need to engage.

How it's done

Using the Three Gs strategy begins with clarification which, as I've stated, is the foundation of all social strategies as far as I'm concerned. Here's an example of a basic Three Gs exchange: "Excuse me, I need directions to get to [insert specific destination here]." I have stated my goal. I have also given the other person information to let him know what my need is. Then I ask a question to communicate the information I need to get: "Do you happen to know where this place is?" If this person doesn't have the information I need, I'll continue asking until I receive it. Once I get the information I need, I close the conversation by saying, "Thank you very much for your help, I really appreciate it."

Now that works great as long I initiate the conversation. But what if someone else initiates it, especially if they initiate chitchat? Remember that the conversation needs to have a goal and a structure. So when a person begins talking to you in a way that leaves her goal unclear to you, you can ask her if there is something specific that she needs. For example, someone says an open-ended pleasantry such as, "Good morning," "What's new?" or something else, and you don't know if she's simply acknowledging you or starting a conversation. So the key is to encourage her to verbalize her intention or purpose. It would sound like this: "Good morning," "Hello, do you need something?" or "Is there something I can do for you?"

Admittedly, a person may be put off by this response because it isn't the rote response we've been socialized to give. When I do this, some people have reacted with surprise and said, "Oh, nothing, I'm just saying hi." This response tells me they were simply acknowledging me. I then respond with, "Thank you."

This next example is kind of fun to use. When a person asks, "What's new?" or "How's it going?" I'll sometimes ask, "How much time have you got? I have this really heavy burden on my conscience and just have to tell someone. Do you have a few hours?" OK, all joking aside, I have said that to people, though. The more practical response is, "Well, there's so much, is there something specific you'd like to know?" If the "What's new?" was one of those greetings not requiring an answer, the person might say, "No, that's OK," or she'll ask a specific question. Either way, you have encouraged her to get to the point so an open-ended potentially chitchatty exchange has now become more focused and concrete.

What if a person responds by saying, "I'm just making conversation." What if they want to make conversation and you don't want to talk? Then by all means let him know that. You can say, "That's very nice of you but I'm rather enjoying just sitting quietly right now."

Practice, practice

You may be thinking that this is all common sense and that you do it already. The point is that many people do in fact do this but they aren't conscious of the steps they're using. It's automatic.

Spectrumites need a purposeful, structured map to follow in order to communicate effectively.

This strategy alone has helped me greatly decrease my social anxiety because it reduces the awkwardness of not knowing what I am going to say. Even the act of saying, "Hi" is a Three Gs conversation. My goal is to acknowledge the other person. What I give them is, "Hi," and what I get in return from them is, "Hi." My goal was to acknowledge the person and get acknowledged. How do I know I effectively accomplished my goal? Because the person said, "Hi" back. Conversation done.

Another way to practice the Three Gs strategy is to use it when you are at a restaurant. I know a lot of kids already know how to do this because they learned it through modeling and insistence by their parents, but they do it in a rote fashion instead of being consciously aware of the steps in the process. When you go to a restaurant, the goal is to get something to eat. The server will come to your table and begin the conversation by stating her goal or purpose for approaching you: "Hi, I'm [so and so], and I'll be your server." Then she needs to get information: "May I get you something to drink?" You, in turn, give her the information requested so she can accomplish the goal of being of service to you. This conversation is very logical, very reciprocal, very win–win and very You, Me, and We.

You can explain the process of the Three Gs to your child so he can conceptualize it and use it deliberately. This will make it easier to generalize to every other conversation. Unless he is conscious of what he's doing, this skill becomes nothing more than restaurant etiquette.

Chapter 11

Asking for Help and Getting It

I want to take a moment to congratulate you for reading this far into the book. It takes great courage to acknowledge when what you're doing in life isn't working. It takes even greater courage to accept your role in how things have become and in how they need to be. You have my utmost respect for taking such bold action to improve your life and the life of those around you. You've been given an opportunity to learn how to improve your communication, to improve the relationships in your life, and you took action, you showed up, and I really want to honor you for that. Too many people continue to suffer in life because they make excuses instead of taking responsibility. Clearly you are not one of those people and I congratulate you on doing that for yourself and those in your life who will benefit from your commitment.

Meltdown at the airport

I want to begin this discussion by sharing the details of an event in my life that speaks to the heart of this chapter, and will serve as an example of the power the strategies in this chapter can have when you need them most. I'm going to be very vulnerable in this example for the benefit of your education. Let me start by saying, "I HATE FLYING." I realize it's a necessary evil as I receive more requests to give presentations out of state. There are the bright lights, echoing overhead announcements, and people repeatedly bumping into me at the airport. Then there are the rapid pressure changes and unpredictable motion of the airplane itself. You'd think that would be enough to send me into a meltdown.

On this occasion I had a very tight schedule. I woke up at 4:30am to get to the airport to fly to a small town in New York State for a presentation that night from 6:30pm to 9:30pm. The landing into the municipal airport had significant turbulence and in addition to praying to God I gripped the seat in front of me so tight that I had a hard time letting go and my hands were stiff and sore.

The rest of the day went smoothly and I did an awesome presentation, met some amazing, generous people, and received some of the best feedback I'd ever had. I was back in my hotel room and resting by 10:30pm. That's a fifteen-hour day with about one hour of downtime in the middle.

I awoke the next morning feeling pretty worn down and very eager to get home to my family. The flight out was fine and I had a layover in Philadelphia before heading home to Chicago. I didn't realize how overloaded and fragile I'd become from my intense schedule until the following happened.

After sitting in the airport for over two hours, about twenty minutes before my flight was supposed to board, they announced that the flight had been canceled because of problems with the plane and they didn't have another plane to replace it. I quickly took out my itinerary and called the discount travel service my client had used to book the flight. The woman who answered was cold, monotone, and clearly following a script. She gave me a thorough explanation of what she couldn't do because of how the flight was booked and "blah blah blah." She told me I had to go to the customer service desk for the airline.

By the time I located customer service the line was at least one hundred people deep and not moving. It was then that someone announced that there were no available flights to Chicago and that we'd have to make overnight accommodations after booking another flight. I began shaking, my eyes began to tear up, all of the sounds in the airport became louder and the lights became more intense as I contemplated having to stand in this hundred-person line for an undetermined amount of time in the hope of getting home. I was beginning to shut down which was making it hard to think and hard to speak. I couldn't think of what to do.

So I did what I encourage every other spectrumite to do in a situation like that. I called for help. Who did I call? My wife Cathy, the most reliable person I've ever known. I explained in my very shaky voice what was happening and how much difficulty I was having even thinking. Cathy, who is a greater gift from God each day that I'm with her, remained very calm and guided me step by step in what to do.

She told me to look for one of the people that transport those with special needs around the airport. I saw one and slowly walked over because I was so shaky I felt like my legs were going to give out. Cathy coached me on what to say because I was having difficulty getting my thoughts together. I think I said something like, "I have autism and they canceled my flight and said they don't have any more flights and I need to get home."

The woman I asked for help is named Shawn and she gently took my bags and told me to sit down in her tramcar because she could hear the tremble in my voice and could see how badly I was shaking. She took my itinerary, asked me a few questions and said she knew someone who could help.

I leaned forward in the seat, stimming with my hands as Shawn navigated her tramcar through a sea of people, as Cathy continued to talk to me and keep me calm. When we stopped Shawn asked if I needed anything and I said no. She said she was going to talk to someone about helping me and she'd be right back. It seemed like an eternity and Cathy kept talking to me. Shawn came back with a gentleman right behind her who handed her a boarding pass with my name on it for a flight that would be leaving an hour and a half later than my original flight was supposed to.

When I was told there were no flights to be had until the next day, Shawn knew I needed a solution. Shawn asked her supervisor Dale for help. He got me a seat on what I later learned was an overbooked flight. When we were seated I was surprised to discover that my seat was in the fourth row so I would be one of the first people off the plane.

A few hours later I was home, sitting on my own couch and contemplating one simple truth that I hope my fellow spectrumites never, ever forget. There is absolutely no value in going through your life stubbornly refusing to ask others for help. I was seconds away from a full-blown meltdown at the airport so I called my wife Cathy who helped me find Shawn. Shawn led me to Dale who helped Shawn help me.

I sat on my own couch, so grateful and humbled to my core by how generously and tenderly I was taken care of by my soulmate and two complete strangers. "Thank you" doesn't even describe it but I'll say it. Thank you, Shawn and Dale at the Philadelphia Airport; you did your employer a tremendous honor by how you conducted yourselves that day.

To my wife Cathy, I will continue to treat you like the gift you are until my last breath. To my fellow spectrumites, as often as I use my own life as an example of who we can be at our strongest—I also want to use my life to demonstrate how absolutely necessary it is to have others in your life who are prepared to help you in your most vulnerable moments. Needing these people isn't a sign of weakness so get that pile of garbage that tells you otherwise from between your ears right now. It is never a sign of weakness, it never was and it never will be. It is, and always will be, the precious gift of service that human beings give to each other.

Speak up

How do you take care of yourself so you're better able to care for others? By asking for help to make sure you get what you need as well. You must make your needs known to those who can meet them. As much as people in general insist that we try and read their minds, that we should know what they think and need, it simply does not happen. Unless you make your needs known, there is no way possible they can get met. Speak up. Then when someone does meet your needs, how might you let them know? Two words. Any ideas?

How about "Thank you"? That is the clearest verification that someone has met your needs effectively. As we both know, self-advocacy is one critical area where spectrumites struggle. What specific task do you think spectrumites struggle with the most when it comes to self-advocacy? You see it in schools all the time, you see it at home when he is trying to do something by himself and is obviously having difficulty. What is it that he will not do? Ask for help. Why do you think that is?

Is it because he doesn't want to feel like he can't do it? Is he too shy to ask for help? Let me ask you this, have you ever had difficulty asking for help? If yes, why? What is the reason for your own reluctance in asking for help? One of the primary reasons spectrumites don't ask for help is because they are often criticized for doing so. Common responses to a request for help are, "Did you try it yourself?" "Did you try before coming to me?" or, "You're not trying hard enough." So, if someone sincerely asks for help and he is discouraged or in any way made to feel bad about it, does that send a message that asking for help is a good idea? Of course it doesn't.

I don't need help

Additional reasons spectrumites don't ask for help are a desire to be independent, and wanting to do it themselves, but the biggest reason I have found that spectrumites do not ask for help is because they are sick and tired of needing so much of it. Does that make sense?

When you think about all the challenges spectrumites have, they go far beyond the social piece most commonly associated with the autism spectrum. Let's say you have gross motor coordination issues and you are clumsy when everyone else seems coordinated. Perhaps it's hard to hold things with your hands and, like me, you're always dropping things unless you have a significantly tight grip on them. Yet everyone else appears to have an easier time with it. The challenges of the autism spectrum impact our relationship with the world in all its aspects, not just with people.

The more difficulty you have, the more help you need, and after a while you just want to feel competent and feel like you can do something. That is what these children, or any human being for that matter, wants most of all: They want the experience of being competent, and the best way to demonstrate that is to do it yourself. The more a child gets frustrated when unable to do it herself, the more that is a window into the child's experience of her own competence. The more adamant she is about doing it herself, the more afraid she is of feeling incompetent. Those are the kids who spend more time feeling disconnected from the world than they feel like they can make anything meaningful happen. Does this clarify things more?

You can look at a child or an adult on the spectrum and say, "She seems so frustrated. Why doesn't she just ask for help?" Because maybe it means that much to her to do it alone, because she spends so much time being unable to do it without help, that asking for help basically equals incompetence, and she may think she's announcing it to the world when she asks for help. We can be so desperate for that feeling of competence that we'll do something twenty times before asking for help in the hope that we'll figure it out and feel like we can solve a problem for once using our own abilities.

I don't know how

In examining my own struggles over the years, as well as conversations with my spectrum clients, I discovered a significant number of them who wanted to ask for help but simply didn't know how. The neurotypicals of the world often do it with ease, but it may not occur to you that asking for help is a complex skill-set with multiple steps involved. It is not a simple ability you're born with.

I presented an in-service for a high school a few years ago, and I'll never forget how blatantly naive a particular teacher was when I brought up the notion that asking for help is a strategy that requires a series of skills. He said, "How hard could it be? You just raise your hand." He also wouldn't accept my explanation as to why it was so difficult for us at times to ask for help when we need it. So I did a lot of thinking in order to figure out what was specifically required to effectively ask for help. I suspected I would encounter others who thought as this teacher did and I'd have to be able to offer more than, "Take my word for it."

What I eventually determined is that there are five main steps involved in asking for help. Without knowing the five steps, many spectrumites will wait for other people to figure out they need help and then get mad when they don't. In exploring this with my clients who knew they needed help but would rather someone else figure it out, I asked, "Why? Why don't you ask for help when you know you need it?" The responses were very telling, "They should know, they can see I need help, and they should just help me." There was a belief among my clients not that others "should" read their minds but that others actually could. Because it was obvious in their minds that help was needed, they assumed others simply knew what they were thinking and decided whether to act or not. Interesting, isn't it?

Of course, we know that that is an absurd expectation of anybody. Unfortunately there are some people so committed to that expectation that they will continue to blame others and say, "I shouldn't have to ask." Still others who know they need help won't ask because they believe their peers will perceive them as stupid. Why do they think that? Because of hearing sniggers and comments from classmates when they ask for help. One young man overheard his friends trash talking the special needs kids and was terrified of being identified as "one of them," even if it meant failing grades. This is what a big deal it is to our kids, especially in an unsupportive and outright predatory school environment.

One way schools attempt to address this challenge but really miss the mark is in how they write IEP goals. If you're unfamiliar with the term, an IEP, or Individualized Education Plan, is the document that spells out the challenge a special needs student has and specifically how it will be accommodated. I have read many IEPs that have goals such as "child will increase her self-advocacy by asking for help when needed." What do goals like this assume about the child? That she knows how to self-advocate.

It is assuming that she knows how and just isn't doing it. When I have brought this to the attention of school staff in IEP meetings, I run into teachers who say the child is intelligent and just needs to ask for help when there is a problem, or the child is not motivated. They come across as quite uninformed about the very students they're being charged with educating. Again, I knew I had to find a way to identify the steps involved in asking for help so I could better explain to spectrumites what and how to do it, as well as educate their teachers on precisely what skills to help their spectrum students develop. So without further ado, here are the five steps for asking for help, as I understand it:

1. You have to know that you need help.

2. You have to know in what form you need the help.

3. You need to know from whom you need help.

4. You need to know how to ask the person for help.

5. You need to know if it's the best time to ask for and receive help.

Step 1

"You have to know that you need help." Can you think of any reasons why you might not know that you need help? You might not even know you are doing something wrong. But how does a person know when he's doing something wrong? Because he examines what he's doing and notes that it's not working or because somebody around him gives him some feedback, perhaps by offering help.

Keep in mind the very common spectrum challenge of connecting with other people. The more difficulty you have connecting, the more it might not occur to you that asking another person is even an option. Maybe you are so disconnected from the world you don't see people as helping solve problems but as creating problems because they are always trying to get into your space, trying to connect with you and talk to you, so if you see people as a problem, you are not going to ask them for help.

Then there are those who insist on doing it themselves, so much in fact they do not want to accept help even when they know they need it. Their basic belief is that they either do it themselves or it can't be done. That would also explain why a lot of them get really mad when things are not working because the only measure of success is for them to do it by themselves.

There is an even bigger reason why spectrumites do not know they need help. And this is a big one. I call parents and teachers out on this all of the time. It occurs when they have a tendency to provide help that was not asked for, or when they constantly run in and rescue the child before he has even had time to realize the problem exists. Have you ever done this?

This is something we are all likely to have done, as we are all very well-meaning parents and we do not want our kids to be sad or hurt, but unfortunately we can't teach them resilience, how to bounce back, or teach them how to fall down and get back up unless they encounter problems. You can't know that you need help with a problem if you don't even know one exists.

The importance of falling down

I only truly learned the value of falling down after going through a rough period in which I had been putting hours upon hours of work into my business and seeing results in the form of a trickle instead of a gush. So I began telling myself a story about what it meant. I began saying how it must be something I did wrong, people must not like me and all other kinds of self-destructive "woe is me" stuff. I had difficulty getting out of this funk so I connected with one of my mentors, Bill. I asked him for help.

Bill is able to spout fountains of wisdom that help me solve my problems even though what he tells me isn't about my problem. What he tells me is more about life. He helped me see the story I was telling myself, and how the facts of the story were focusing on people who weren't coming through, business relationships that were fizzling out, promises that weren't kept, and goals that were not yet realized.

Then he helped me look again at the rest of my story: my story as a twenty-two-year cancer survivor, an undaunted advocate for my children, the spectrum community, and myself. The more he helped remind me of the entirety of my story instead of my fixation on this small span of time the more I realized that my whole life story has been about falling down, and more importantly about getting back up.

In that moment I realized my whole life, my business, my parenting, everything, is about getting back up and moving forward. I discussed this realization with him and we discussed how our lives and the whole of the human experience is about falling down and getting back up. Those of us who become the ones others look to for help when they're down are the ones who have become very skilled in the art of getting back up.

I've listened over the years to the self-help gurus who don't talk about their falls. They come off as larger than life, indestructible success machines. I have learned very little from them because they talk more about being up all the time. My experience begins with the fall. What I need to know is how to stand back up. It does me little good to know how to be up all the time when I don't know how to get there. Even worse is when we're given the impression that falling is failure when in fact falling is critical. The more falls we have the more options we have for getting back up and the more we have to teach others.

I recall my dysfunctional upbringing (many of us have one of those) and recall the times I was laughed at for falling. My insecure father would mockingly say, "I saw that." A habit my siblings picked up. I would be laughed at by peers for tripping, criticized in gym class by teachers and other students for my clumsiness.

But in each and every case, I got back up. It's difficult to remember that very important part while the focus is on the fall. Far too many people focus so much on falling down that they stay down. My funk during this period was due to putting my focus on the fall, or what I perceived as a fall, instead of focusing on getting back up. So from now on, when someone sees you fall and makes fun of you, think of this. When I feel myself fall, I will meet that experience with the following words: "Now watch me get back up." This is the lesson our spectrumites need to learn but they must be allowed to fall before they can learn it.

What isn't working?

This brings up some important questions. How do you teach children to know that they need help when they either want to do it themselves no matter what, or want you to read their minds, or don't consider asking people for help as an option? Tough questions, huh?

For some, it amounts to helping them realize it's more important for them to solve the problem than to solve it alone. Part of that discussion involves choosing how many times is enough before asking for help. Having that concrete benchmark is very helpful.

Another approach, when you are observing a child or adult who seems to be doing something over and over again and not getting anywhere, is to ask what I have found to be the million-dollar question for checking in and giving him the opening or opportunity to ask for help. This is a strategy that comes up often in my trainings. The question is: "Is something not going the way it's supposed to?"

I say this to my boys and hear responses such as, "Yes, this is stupid," or, "This stupid thing isn't working." Then I ask, "What is it supposed to be doing?" I hear some variation of how it's supposed to be working. Now listen closely to how I ask the question because words matter. You could ask it this way: "What problem are you having right now?" or even, "What isn't going the way you want it to?" What I have found in talking to spectrum kids who are used to a lot of criticism, is that just by throwing the word "you" in there, he can hear it as a criticism, because he hears that you are talking about him having a problem and that he is the one messing up. I know that choosing your words so carefully can seem a lot like walking on egg shells, and sometimes it is, but when you have children who are so used to being criticized, they come to believe that where there's a problem, it has something to do with them not being good enough somehow. I have found that it helps when you phrase the question in this way: "What isn't going the way it's supposed to?" You are referring to what isn't working in the situation instead of what isn't working with him.

Now here's something important to keep in mind. Sometimes a child who is used to criticism from an adult will miss how carefully you chose your words and default to thinking the statement was about him. So if you say, "Is something not going the way it's supposed to?" and he replies, "I'm not *stupid*," then you need to clarify for him what you were actually referring to. For example, "OK, let me clarify. I didn't say you were stupid; in fact, I think you're very intelligent. I was just wondering what isn't working here in this situation." So you need to reiterate that you are talking about the situation, not about him. Depending on how defensive a child is it may take some time for him to begin to hear and appreciate the difference. Not only in how you see the situation, but also in beginning to see it the same way. Then, after being clear that you're talking about the situation, you can ask, "What needs to happen to make it go the way it is supposed to?" Again, talking about what the situation needs in order to change. I want to reassure you that once you get used to seeing the situation in this way, speaking in this new way becomes very natural.

Beliefs matter

What really makes the difference is when you believe that the problem really is about the situation, and not the child. The words you use now show what your beliefs are. There's one belief behind the question, "What's your problem?" And an entirely different belief behind the question, "What's the problem?" A belief shift that can make a world of difference in how you relate to your child and how your child relates to herself.

Your beliefs determine more than how you perceive a problem; they also determine the options you believe are available for solving the problem. If you believe you must do it yourself, you might not believe that the option of asking another person for help even exists. If you believe the child's attitude is the problem you relieve yourself of the option and responsibility of doing anything differently to help her make any changes. Your beliefs determine your options and therefore the actions you take. The biggest belief shift is in whether taking action, in this case asking for help, causes more problems than it solves. If asking for help means you have just announced to the world that you are incompetent yet again, then why on earth would you ask for it? But if asking for help solves the problem of making this situation work and it is not a reflection upon you at all, then asking for help is a lot easier to do because it's a more pleasing option. It is a matter of changing your belief and thus your viewpoint on asking for help, changing it from a sign of failure and helplessness to a sign of intelligence.

A specific belief that's helpful to adopt in order to make this shift is, "I ask for help because I am brave enough to take on tasks that require more than one brain and more than two hands." Does that work for you? It means you are taking on bigger challenges and are more confident and can handle big things, but this task happens to require a little more than you can do alone, so you will ask for help. Therefore, you are walking into a situation knowing you need and want help as opposed to walking into it believing you must do it yourself.

Another belief is, "A problem solved alone may take forever. A problem is solved more quickly when solved together." Spend some time seriously considering those beliefs until they're ingrained in your thinking. This completes Step 1: "You have to know that you need help."

Step 2

"You have to know in what form you need the help." Once a person has determined that he needs help, he has to determine in what form he needs it. Does he need information that can be acquired simply by asking a question and having it answered? Does he need to have something specifically demonstrated, or assistance in doing it? This is important for spectrumites to know; otherwise, his request won't be specific enough. Simply saying, "I need help," "I'm stuck," or "I don't get it" isn't enough.

We have different learning styles, and some learn better visually by seeing, auditorily by hearing, or kinesthetically by touching or doing. One common disconnect I see, especially in classrooms, is a visual learner who has an auditory teacher. The visual student wants to see graphics, pictures, handouts, and overheads, while the teacher wants to talk, explain, and lecture. This teacher is baffled by the student's claim that, "The teacher doesn't help me." The reality is that the teacher's way of helping isn't effective because of this disconnect in learning and teaching styles. This would also explain why a student who ordinarily does very well in one subject suddenly begins doing poorly—one thing to consider is whether the teaching style has changed. Imagine how many problems could be solved if you could just figure out how a student learned and teach accordingly. One problem I want to validate is the difficulty a teacher has accommodating such a specific learning style when responsible for a classroom of individual students.

Another thing I want to address is the stereotype that people on the spectrum are visual learners. In reality it is not true. Many of them, including some who are nonverbal, are auditory learners. I have met or read about spectrumites who were assumed to have a low IQ because they were being taught and tested visually. Once it was discovered they learned better auditorily or kinesthetically, everything changed. I am suspicious of testing in general for people on the spectrum because of the unique differences among them. Any professional performing a standardized test on people who are often so different in how they take in information can make one person appear gifted and another extremely limited, depending on how the person is tested.

For yourself and for the sake of your child, you need to know how you learn best as well to decrease this disconnect between the two of you as much as possible. Once you know what your learning style is, you then need to deliberately use the language of that style when you make requests for help. Remember, words matter. Here are some examples:

- Can you show me how?

- Can you tell me how?

- Can I watch you do it?

Asking questions that way, according to your learning style, gives the other person a clue as to what you are looking for.

Step 3

"You need to know from whom you need help." When you ask for help, it needs to be from a person who actually has what you need. Spectrumites tend to want to ask everything of the person they are most comfortable with even if that person repeatedly demonstrates that she doesn't have the information. One client I worked with was a young man who loved everything about World War II. Could not get enough of it, couldn't talk enough about it. This child would go to his parents when he couldn't understand something he was reading and wanted an explanation. He would ask his mother, "Why did the general do this? What was he thinking? Why didn't he do it this way?" And his mother would reply, "Honestly, son, I have no idea." And he would get angry at her because she didn't know. He wanted the answer but he wanted it from somebody he was comfortable asking or who was convenient to ask as opposed to the person who could actually answer the question. Have you encountered this?

Where are the answers?

The fact of the matter is that the child or adult on the spectrum is probably asking a very reasonable question of exactly the wrong person, so it is important to help her identify the key people and resources to help find the answers she needs. I am always leading my three spectrumites toward finding the solutions beyond me so they get used to working with other people or having other resources. When one of them asks a question that I don't know the answer to, I will let him know that I don't know and ask how we might go about finding the answer together. We will brainstorm the options we have to help him learn to discover the various ways of finding the answer. If he can't get it from me, it's generally on the internet, so what search engines do we want to use or websites do we want to check out?

Maybe we can think about the people we know who might have the information. My wife is really big on taking the boys to the library to look things up; the day they got their library cards they were so excited you'd think we had given them each a credit card with a million-dollar limit. That is the beauty of having children who love information. Getting them library cards was beautiful, and it is also a wonderful way to get them to leave the house and explore. The library is also a great place to practice self-advocacy because what if you can't find what you're looking for? Whom do you have to ask? A librarian. You have to ask somebody else. It is a wonderful opportunity to practice these steps: What else do I need, whom do I ask, and how do I need it?

Step 4

"You need to know how to ask the person for help." Depending on whom you need to ask, it may require walking up to him and asking in person, or it might require sending an e-mail, making a phone call, texting, or whatever way you and he agree is the best way to communicate with each other. I know many spectrumites who do not like using the phone. They just won't do it. I, for one, prefer e-mail and I use the phone only when absolutely necessary. Do you know anyone who does not like the phone or who prefers one means of communication to another?

Why do we hate using the phone?

For some on the spectrum, the use of the telephone is such a tremendous source of anxiety that they'd rather do without than use the phone. For the record, my wife and I both hate using the phone. Many of my clients prefer using video conferencing because they hate using the phone. So what's the big deal? Here are several reasons.

Surprise

For spectrumites, socialization, as you know, is difficult and is something we often put a lot of thought into doing. We need to prepare our opening line, decide what we want to talk about, etc.

So when a phone suddenly rings we're expected to simply answer it with no preparation time. I've told my clients repeatedly to e-mail me, let me get my thoughts together and I'll call them back, preferably I'll e-mail them back. Needless to say I use voicemail a lot.

Pauses

Phone conversations contain a pressure to keep talking. Pauses aren't easy to come by. When you're physically with someone you can enjoy each other's company without talking. On the phone you must talk. For spectrumites who have a delay between choosing the words in their mind and then speaking them, the pressure to keep the phone conversation moving can be too great.

Pacing

The invention of e-mail and texting has been a godsend for many spectrumites, including myself. We can now choose our words carefully and have exchanges in short bursts instead of in lengthy phone conversations that usually involve listening to a lot of extraneous information that has nothing to do with the point. With e-mail and texting we can cut to the chase, state the facts and get on with it.

Patience

We also don't know if the person we have to call will have the patience to work with us as we take our time and find the words to communicate what we need and how we need it. The fear of appearing foolish to someone who doesn't know you can be so great that you'd rather do without than make the call.

I have a few clients who fare much better in a conversation if they text their response, even if the person is in front of them. It is much easier for them to get the words out and get them out quickly if they do it that way instead of speaking. With that in mind, what if you need to ask for help from somebody and the only available option is face-to-face speaking? That's a problem if you're uncomfortable with that medium, and even more so if you're nonverbal. In this instance, having a means to write your request would be helpful. My middle son does that a lot.

What's your style?

In many cases, the barrier isn't the means of communication, spoken or written, but the style of communication. I remember a specific event from my own life. It was many years ago, before I knew I was on the spectrum. I was working for a hospice as a social worker and visiting a patient in a nursing home. I approached a nurse but offered no greeting or pleasantry—I just began asking her a question. She stepped back and said, "Well, good morning to you, too." Her response threw me off because I was focused on getting my question answered. When she responded that way, I was rattled for a few seconds and then realized that she wanted me to greet her. So I collected myself and I said, "Good morning" and asked her if she had a moment, and fortunately she said she did. Now that I had given her what she wanted, she was happy to answer my question. In that instance I was asking the right question of the right person, but my style was too abrupt for her and threw her off. She gave me feedback, I adjusted, and I got my question answered.

Have you encountered style issues when interacting with spectrumites? As a parent, are you told your child is rude or blunt? In college I was often told that I was too blunt, rude, and insensitive. I thought all I was doing was answering the questions asked of me. I was just being honest.

So even when you know that you have a problem, know how to ask, know the way you need it, and even know the person to ask, if your style throws the person off, it can definitely be a barrier to getting help.

Rehearsal

Allow me to offer a suggestion to help overcome a style issue. The way that I do it is I rehearse it. When I say, "rehearse," I do not mean role-playing. I am not a particular fan of role-playing because it gives the false impression that the other person is going to do what the person you role-played with did, and if the real situation does not go that way, you might get thrown off or freeze in the actual conversation. It makes it difficult. When I say, "rehearse," I mean your part of it—your side. In the case of a phone call, I write down what I want to say before I even start dialing. I do this a lot when I have to call tech support for any kind of computer glitch, because I get a little rattled talking to someone I don't have a rapport with. So I write down the questions I have, and then practice asking them until I'm comfortable.

E-mail is a wonderful alternative. You can take your time responding and choose your words carefully. E-mail eliminates the anxiety over trying to get the words out, or using the right vocal tone or facial expression; you can just focus on the statements you want to make and the questions you want answered.

Rehearsing is helpful when you need to see a person face to face. Rehearse it in front of a mirror, in your mind, or out loud, so you can clearly think out what you want to say, what you want to ask beforehand. I use this strategy to this day. Most social situations are unstructured and unpredictable, I am outside my element and need to really think things through and think about what I'm going to do and say, and it helps me focus, be more confident and more comfortable, and prevents me from becoming tongue-tied. That is one of the reasons why I prefer e-mail, because if the phone rings and I have to answer it and I am not ready to have a conversation, I will freeze. I will have a slight anxiety attack. I prefer it to go to voicemail, and then I can listen to what the person wants and call him back once I rehearse what I am going to say.

Step 5

"You need to know if it's the best time to ask for and receive help." It is possible that you have the right question, you have worded it in the right way, you are asking the person in the way that you need it, and you have the right person, but it is not the most convenient time to ask that person. Here's an example of how you can resolve a possible issue of timing when asking for help: "Hello, I have something I need some help with. Is now a good time for you?"

The alternative is the one I described earlier, in which a spectrumite will simply burst in and start having a conversation without even checking in with you. Without considering the issue of timing, as spectrumites we run the risk of interrupting or distracting the person by simply talking about what we want. If she becomes upset with you, it could result in her not wanting to help you. If you do interrupt and she cuts you off, what becomes your experience of asking for help? You learn that when asking for help, people get mad at you. So even when you have the first four steps in order, not accounting for timing can blow everything. That is why all five steps are essential. "Is this a good time?" "Do you have a moment?" If the answer is yes, hurray! You can continue with your question. If it is no, then you need to know when is a good time and you can ask her when a better time would be. Then you can follow up with her and get the help you need.

Let me recap the five steps before we move on. The five steps for asking for help are:

1. You have to know that you need help.

2. You have to know in what form you need the help.

3. You need to know from whom you need help.

4. You need to know how to ask the person for help.

5. You need to know if it's the best time to ask for and receive help.

Touch and Go

A teacher asked me how to teach these steps to young children. He shared that he can tell when one of his students needs a sensory break but does not ask for it. (A sensory break is time away from the classroom during which a child has an opportunity for sensory input such as swinging, deep pressure, lying down, etc., that allows the child to decompress the stress of being in the classroom.) The strategy I explained to him that he could negotiate with this child is one I call Touch and Go. Touch and Go is a process that I use that allows me to spend time in a sensory intense setting such as a classroom, a restaurant, or a wedding without melting down or getting totally overloaded. Touch and Go means I touch base with a person in that environment, and let the person know I'm taking a break and then I go. I take breaks in order to calm down and prevent overload before I go back into the environment until I need to touch base again.

I've experienced an unfortunate precedent being set with spectrumites in the classroom setting. They sometimes receive a mixed message when it comes to taking care of themselves. Whereas their IEP allows for sensory breaks, and parents and teachers tell the students to ask for them when needed, on occasion the reality is that they're actively discouraged by school staff because of losing valuable class time, teaching time, whatever. What's even worse is that the child's request may be met with frustration such as, "You need to learn how to cope better," or "Wait until we're done with this lesson." Have you experienced this?

If as an educator you respond to a student's request for a break by asking him to be patient, I want to make something very clear. A spectrumite who is expending his energy on holding it together in your classroom isn't learning much and is, in fact, missing valuable teaching time simply by being in your room. So by discouraging him from using breaks, you are telling him not to take care of himself.

You reinforce the experience that a classroom is a place where needs don't get met, making it an even more difficult place to be in, Telling him to learn to cope better encourages a sense of shame and failure around acknowledging that he's getting overloaded and needs to get out of there and get a break. If you want to encourage him to learn self-advocacy, then honor asking for a break as a successful demonstration of a coping strategy instead of the absence of one.

What if you radically change your approach as a parent or a teacher and the child still refuses to take a break when it's offered and won't ask for one? What he's probably being influenced by is a belief that taking a break is a sign of weakness. Explore this possibility by asking if he thinks taking a break is a bad thing and see what he says. Until he sees taking a break as a positive way of taking care of himself instead of something that will cause him social disapproval, he'll be highly conflicted over it. He'll feel like he needs it but also feel bad about needing it. That's a lousy place to be in experientially.

It's crucial for spectrumites to be able to use Touch and Go, and it's just as important to have those in their lives support it and support their use of it. It has been a tremendous asset to me in my adult life, and I will admit there are times when I was not true to myself and didn't use it when I needed to.

Ignoring the signs

About a week after Cathy and I were married I was to meet her extended family for the first time at Thanksgiving dinner. I'd met many of them already, in smaller numbers, and they were welcoming and kind. However, after Cathy informed me there would be nearly fifty people at Thanksgiving dinner I was overwhelmed with anxiety. Cathy noticed I was nervous and when she inquired I said, "I don't know what to do there." It was more than not knowing the protocol of the event; I also didn't know how to cope with such an intense environment.

I grew up in a family of spectrumites and Thanksgiving with my family reflected that. We'd sit in a room together and there was no pressure to talk to each other until dinner. Each of us had an activity we were engaged in, from reading a book to watching TV, and we were content with that. In fact, to be in a room with so many others who understand this way of being together was comforting. Dinner conversation consisted of very select bullet points and then we would sit around a while longer and go home.

Cathy's family is very large, and very social. We spent the week before discussing the protocol, the people who would be there and my options for getting away if I needed to decompress. I had several sleepless nights as I fretted over all of the unknowns. Thanksgiving day arrived; my sons spent the day with other relatives, while Cathy and I spent a quiet morning together before going to her aunt's house where everyone would be gathering.

We arrived early to help set up which would give me more time to familiarize myself with the space and adjust as people began to arrive. The more people arrived, the busier and louder it got and the more my anxiety rose. I soon found myself on the heated patio sitting in a chair far from the door and afraid to leave the room. Cathy checked on me and asked if I was OK. I replied with my original concern, "I don't know what the rules are. I don't know what to do." Unfortunately, all the plans and rehearsal in the world under ideal circumstances does not prepare a spectrumite for the disorganizing intensity of the actual situation. So our week of planning for this moment turned out to be of little value.

I was blessed in that this dear, sweet angel who was my wife of one week now stayed close to me the entire time. She agreed to act as a buffer and bring to me those who wanted to meet me so I could experience them in doses instead of droves. I was able to loosen up and crack a few jokes as a few of the more familiar relatives sat at our table and we engaged in friendly conversation.

I was getting tired but felt more relaxed. When we moved to the larger room for dessert, it was like slamming into a wall. It was louder, brighter, and contained several very young children who were reaching their saturation point as well. Their inconsolable crying was evidence of it. I was able to tune out for a few minutes while sampling a piece of the most incredible homemade pumpkin pie I'd ever eaten.

Not long after that I was snapped to attention when Cathy placed her hand on my shoulder. I was completely tuned out and shutting down when she did that and of course didn't realize it. She asked, "Are you ready to go?" I remember telling her a few times that I was OK (when I wasn't) and encouraging her to enjoy herself. I would then shut down again. The last time she checked in with me, she gently placed her hand on my shoulder and when she had my attention she said, "I'm ready to go." She took responsibility for saying it was time and took the pressure off me.

We said a few quick goodbyes and as we walked down the driveway she explained that she could tell I'd had enough of the situation and asked why I hadn't said anything sooner. She added that we didn't have to stay. I said that I didn't want to be a party pooper and ruin her time with her family. This episode reminded me just how much I have constructed a life of familiarity around myself. I live a life in which I've successfully protected myself from situations that overwhelm me. It had been years since I walked into a situation where I felt paralyzed and helpless because there were more unknowns than knowns.

Whereas today I find myself in situations where many look to me to lead, this was one of many situations where it was necessary for me to follow the lead of those who knew the rules and could help keep me safe. This is a vulnerability few people understand. Though Cathy and I had discussed and agreed to use Touch and

Go, I wasn't confident enough in that environment to use it and paid the price.

No place to go

Another teacher explained that one of the challenges at her school is that it doesn't have many quiet places for students to go and calm down if they are feeling overloaded. She asked for suggestions on how to accommodate students under these circumstances.

I explained to her that before she could accommodate them she needs to know what calms each student in question. If unable to go to a different place, it is possible to use Touch and Go by doing something different in the same place. Have you ever encountered a child who listens best while pacing in the back of the room? How about a student who does better standing at her desk?

These are examples of how a spectrumite can experience calming sensory input by interacting with the space differently when a different location isn't readily available. However, as with my middle son, a different, quieter place may be necessary. So if you don't have a different place for the student to go, you need to do some detective work and find out why he's getting overloaded in that place to begin with, and maybe the problem can be solved right there by modifying the environment. In the case of a child who's more kinesthetic, one of the biggest challenges with the expectation of sitting still, with eyes front, not talking to his neighbor, and listening to his teacher is that you're denying him the very thing he needs in order to stay organized. He needs to move.

When you deny him this, you make being in the classroom a source of pain. However, when you negotiate how and where he can move when needed, in the back of the room as opposed to back and forth in front of the teacher, then he can move when needed with your full support. As long as he can pace in the back of the classroom, he can hear everything you are saying and can take it in in an organized way.

In terms of Touch and Go in my case, since I am very auditory, if I go to a place that is very noisy, my first line of defense is earplugs; cheap, easy-to-use, foam earplugs can make a world of difference in terms of allowing me to withstand a noisy environment for probably twice as long as I would have without them. The result is that I need to Touch and Go less frequently. Earplugs make it easier to hear only the person I'm talking to. Since too many sounds in an environment, whether loud or not, can be overwhelming, earplugs make the other sounds harder to hear, making talking to one person easier.

Somebody who is touch sensitive and doesn't like people brushing up against her may prefer to stay on the periphery where she can see people coming as opposed to being in the mix. I do this as a matter of course because of my touch sensitivity. When in a restaurant, I want a seat where I can see who is coming at me; at a party, I will try and get there first; at a movie theater, I will get there early so I can find the seating where I can see people coming. I can find a seat where people are not going to be walking in front of me and brushing against me. So that is one way to prepare yourself in your environment so you can interact and minimize the things that will overload you.

Those with visual and motion sensitivity will look down a lot in crowded situations because the floor doesn't move and looking at a stable surface helps them keep their balance. You'll see me looking at the ground when I walk for that reason.

Social disclaimers

That's a lot to go through to avoid being overloaded, so here's the simplest way I've found to implement Touch and Go even with people you've just met. It's through a strategy I call Social Disclaimers.

When you think of a disclaimer, it is typically in the form of a warning label: If you use this hair dryer in the shower, it's not our fault if you get electrocuted. In other words, expect it. It is a denial of responsibility by the manufacturer if you use the product in a way that is likely to result in harm. But I think of a Social Disclaimer as a spectrumite relieving himself of the responsibility of doing something that may ordinarily be expected, such as eye contact, shaking hands, and hugging, because it causes him difficulty that would be at the expense of effective communication.

Even if those things are expected, if doing them causes you extreme discomfort or overload, you need to reserve the right not to do them. But you also need to self-advocate and let others know that you're reserving this right; you can even do so without disclosing that you're on the autism spectrum. Though I have been told time and time again that such things as eye contact and handshakes are nonnegotiable, the reality is that in many situations with very inflexible rules of engagement, they can be made flexible with a social disclaimer. I have found that most people will respect your desire not to practice expected social conventions when they understand why.

The idea that eye contact is absolutely necessary for communication is a bunch of nonsense. Blind people have communication. They have close relationships and they do not look you in the eye. Let me ask you this: Is it possible for someone to look you in the eye and not hear a word you're saying? Yes it is, so how useful is eye contact as a means of knowing that someone is paying attention to you? It isn't reliable at all.

How do you know if someone truly heard you? Ask, clarify, that's the only way to know for sure. So get over the eye contact issue. Some of us need to listen with our ears only or we'll miss what you're saying. That is definitely the case with me. I can look at you or I can listen to you but I cannot give you both. Here's an example of how I use a Social Disclaimer to allow myself the option of not making eye contact. I will say, "It's pretty noisy in here and it's a lot easier for me to hear you if I tilt my ear towards you." When I say that, I have just let her know that I am not going to look at her, why, and how she'll know I'm listening. I do not have to say I am on the autism spectrum, or that I have sensory difficulties. I just explain that I hear better when I turn my ear towards her.

Handshaking is a big issue for me as well so I have learned to initiate a knuckle bump to avoid the awkwardness of someone extending his hand for a shake, only to have me avoid it. Each person responds differently to this approach. People my age or older sometimes appear as though they don't know what I'm doing. Those younger than me get it more quickly and don't seem to mind it.

I also have a Social Disclaimer that allows others to help me monitor my tendency to monologue. When we begin talking about a subject I really like, I proclaim, "Sometimes I get a little long-winded, and if I do that, feel free to interrupt me if you want to say something." With this disclaimer, I've described something I have difficulty doing, and told him how he can deal with it if it happens and also meet his own need to say something when he wants to without getting annoyed with me or feeling rude for interrupting me. I've stated the problem, the solution I need, the form I need it in, and from whom I need it. I did it in a single statement.

Of course, this flies in the face of most social skills classes that insist you need to look at a person's face and need to know if he's bored or wants to change the subject. You also need to remember to pause and ask the other person if he would like to say something. You know, some days we remember to do that, but a large percentage of the time, especially when nervous, we forget to do all of those things. A disclaimer is only a single thing to remember, and you can begin with it.

A Social Disclaimer lets you enlist the other person in helping you by asking him to verbalize what he needs when he needs it. Then when he does what you've asked, you can say thank you and let him talk. See how much easier that is? Neurotypical social skills classes don't teach things like this because they insist that communication has to be what works for them instead of what works for the two people having the conversation.

Are you getting a massive headache from everything I have just poured into your head? I understand that some may be able to apply this immediately while others need to take more time and let it sink in. It is a belief shift, after all. When you are able to make the shift, you will think differently and you will do differently. These strategies are to help spectrumites engage with the world more effectively by meeting it halfway, instead of having to experience social encounters as a multitasking nightmare that far too often teeters on the edge of disaster.

Chapter 12

From Rejection to Resilience

This chapter will focus on one of the most common and hurtful experiences of the autism spectrum: rejection. For many of us, rejection feels more like the rule than the exception. For the vast majority of us, the pain of repeated rejection turns us into big balls of anxiety that compel us to react, sometimes aggressively, to even the slightest disappointment. Though I understand this response, I also understand that it needs to change. This is a response that guarantees further rejection since it also serves to push away the very people most eager to help us.

The one word in the human language that seems to be the all-purpose trigger for this storehouse of anxiety and hurt is the word *no*. I suspect you know what can happen when you say that word to a spectrumite. What I will explain in this chapter is how to teach your child to hear the word *no* without falling apart, melting down, or feeling rejected.

Filling in the gaps

Repairing deep emotional wounds in any person, especially a spectrumite, can't be done with a pill or some other fly-by-night, quick-fix technique. It can only occur through renegotiating your relationship in a way that takes an individual's emotional triggers into consideration and makes an effort to side-step them. By doing so you can reduce the likelihood the spectrumite you're interacting with will react the same old way to disappointment which can make further communication very difficult.

The first strategy I'd like to discuss goes all the way back to the invention of questions themselves and was turned into a simple system by journalists in order to get the essential facts of the story they were eager to report. Through asking six simple questions— Who, What, When, Where, Why, and How—they were and are able to get a complete picture of the subject at hand. This allows you to have what I refer to as a 360 degree conversation. By making sure the information you provide, and ask for, answers each of these questions, you can significantly increase the likelihood that all necessary information is communicated in a concrete manner instead of being implied.

I recently taught this approach to a mother who was very frustrated with her son. She stated that she'd tell him what to do five or six times and he'd stare at her blankly. She'd give him advice on how to use social strategies at school, and he wouldn't do them. I'll describe a common exchange between them to demonstrate what I mean. Let's call the son John and the mother Mary.

Mary said, "I explained to John over and over again that all he has to do at school is walk up to somebody he wants to talk to, introduce himself, and ask if they want to play. It is so simple and yet he doesn't do it."

Have you ever given similar instruction to your child? Encouraging them to, "Just get out there and do it," or, "You need to stop being so anxious and just do it." I know many parents who have done this, and I'm sure I have done it as well in the past.

Now with the 360 degree approach in mind, let's revise Mary's statement to John: "All you have to do is walk up to somebody and ask to play, that's all you need to do." If that is the instruction that John is getting, let's review the six necessary questions to see what information he actually has.

Who: Refers to the people who are the subject of the discussion, in this case, Mary, John, and whoever the child is that John is supposed to approach.

What: What John is being encouraged to do, which is introduce himself and ask to play.

Where: School is the place he's being encouraged to do this.

When: We don't know when. School lasts around six hours, during which there are various opportunities to talk to another classmate about playing together. John does not know when to make this request based on the advice Mary is giving him. There are too many variables.

How: John doesn't know this either. "Just walk up, introduce yourself, and ask to play" ignores many other things John needs to know how to do.

Then there is the matter of Why? "Why do I want to do this again, Mom? Why can't I just play alone? Why would I want to just walk up to somebody and ask them to play?" Those questions have not been answered. Those gaps have not been filled in. He doesn't have enough information to work with. Based on Mary's insistence that he just walk up to somebody and ask him to play, what do you think Mary's goals are for John in this situation?

Perhaps it's as simple as wanting him to meet his classmates and have what she considers to be typical interactions with them. Again, why would he want to meet some people if he is content playing by himself all the time? Mary explained that, "He seems so lonely and humans are social creatures, so he needs to interact with people."

There's no arguing with our need for other people in our lives. But if meeting them were as simple as Mary is explaining it to John, then why aren't more people on the spectrum rushing out to make friends? Because it's so difficult to do, there are too many unknowns. With this in mind, when Mary's goal is for John to meet other people, what do you think John's goals are for himself? Do you think John just wants to do his own thing? If that's what he's used to doing, and interacting with others is so difficult, does it make sense that John would simply choose the path of least resistance?

As it turns out, John's experience with his peers has been overwhelmingly negative. So in his mind, the idea of reaching out to them is an invitation for rejection. He has repeatedly been told that he's weird, that the other kids don't like him, and to stay away.

So many questions

In terms of the six questions that need to be answered, there may be numerous questions that John is asking quietly in his mind in response to Mary's suggestion that he simply go introduce himself and ask to play. These questions need to be answered to help John fill in the gaps, to reduce the number of unknowns regarding how to effectively go into that situation and accomplish his main goal. Questions such as:

- Who am I supposed to talk to?

- How do I choose to approach?

- What are we supposed to play together?

- When am I supposed to introduce myself?

- How do I say it?

- How do I do that again?

- Why can't I just play alone?

- Why is this a big deal?

All these questions and more are going through John's head, and they are not being answered. Mary is certainly not answering them because she doesn't even realize that John doesn't have the information she does, to her it's common sense. When neither the parent nor child is able to identify the unknowns, the spectrumite is essentially on his own.

So in order to make sure you have provided all or as much of the information your child needs as possible, use the six questions to inform the advice you give and review the advice once you've given it to make sure you've covered everything.

Using the Ws

Here's an example of how I used the six questions to prepare myself for an unpredictable situation. My family and I decided to go to the public water park, with lots of people, noise, and everything that I typically avoid. This is something my wife typically does with them but this time they were begging me to come along. I hadn't been to this pool before, and I felt my anxiety level increase the closer we got because there were so many unknowns. Unknowns, of course, drive anxiety. The more unknowns there are, the more anxiety there is. So I began asking myself the questions and answering them to calm myself down. I said, "OK, what are we going to do? We are going to swim. Where are we going? We are going to the pool, and I know where it is. When are we going to get there? How long are we going to stay? Why are we going? Because we are going to have fun, so I get to see the kids and hear them laugh. I get to support the kids. What kinds of things am I going to do there? What kinds of things will make me nervous there that I want to stay away from? What if I get overheated? Where is the shade?" And the more knowns I created for myself, the more prepared I felt and the more I calmed down.

Another way to use these questions is when you have to take your child with you to run errands. Your child needs predictability and structure to her experience in order to feel safe and calm. So you can prepare her by providing answers to the questions: Where are we going? How long are we going to be there? When are we going to get home? She is already asking these questions in her mind whether she asks them out loud or not. When you run through the questions in your own mind it will probably help you recall information you have not told her yet. For example, "I plan on going [wherever you're going], too, but I forgot to mention that. Thanks for reminding me, honey. By the way, we are going to go [wherever], also."

It's easy to forget when you're in a rush, but using these questions as a framework helps you slow down and organize your thinking. You can prevent yourself and your child from feeling that anxiety just by running through the list in your head, sharing the answers with your child and getting on the same page.

When it comes to social skills trainings, I have seen our kids instructed in the same way Mary instructed John. Typically the assumption is that it is going to go well, the other child will accept, and everyone will play happily ever after together. I rarely hear it presented with the possibility that the other child might say no. I've heard the spectrumite ask that question, only to be told, "You need to be more positive." That response doesn't solve that problem. Only a strategy will. It's irresponsible to dismiss the legitimate questions our kids ask themselves even when we feel they're negative. When you find a way to answer the questions and solve the problems, then they aren't problems anymore.

So your child may be asking herself:

- What if the other person says no?

- What if I mess it up?

- What if the other person makes fun of me?

- And heaven forbid, what if the person says yes? Then what happens next?

You need to have answers. All Mary was offering John was the suggestion to go introduce himself and ask to play. What if the other kid says yes, then what am I supposed to do? That's an even bigger issue for the child. It's fair to say that one of the reasons John is not following Mary's advice is because every time he has taken Mary's advice in the past, it didn't work, so why would he put himself out there again? He might be thinking

- "Why do I need friends when all they do is tease me and criticize me?"

- "Why should I take her advice when it hasn't worked before?"

- "What's the point?" (He feels ineffective; that's why he doesn't want to keep doing it.)

What good is encouraging your child over and over again to go out there and take social risks and make friends when your child has all the questions going on in his mind, questions such what if I look bad, what if they call me a jerk? Your encouragement can't compete with that. So, how do you help a child thinking this way to overcome it? Not sure?

You begin by realizing that if your child doesn't believe that your advice will solve the problem, he won't do it. In the scenario with John, he sees Mary's advice as opening himself up to further criticism and rejection. So what we need to do is get at John's core belief about this request. Why isn't he doing it and what does he believe about it? In order to shift his thinking from looking at this as an opportunity to make friends, instead of a danger to avoid, Mary needs to know how to talk to him to find out what his belief is.

Let me walk you through how that discussion might sound. Mary would say, "John, I would like to talk to you about something so you can help me understand it better."

What do you think about this opening statement? Does she have John's attention? Would he think he is in trouble? Beginning the statement with his name is the most efficient way to get his attention. It also asks for his assistance in helping Mary understand something, which puts him in the position of the expert who will be helping somebody older than him.

He hears that he is the one with the answers, while usually he is the one who is being lectured and told what to do and told he's doing it wrong. But now Mary says she would like him to help her understand something. Here is an opportunity for John to feel competent. That is a wonderful way to open up this conversation with any child.

The next statement Mary is going to make is: "John, when I give you suggestions about how to make friends at school, I don't feel I have been helping you as well as I could. I would like to be more helpful to you. In order to do that, I need to ask you some questions. Is that OK?"

What do you think about the explanation Mary gave? Is there anything missing from it? Actually, all six questions have been answered; it is a complete statement. Let me show you how.

- Who: John and Mary.

- What: Give suggestions on making friends at school.

- When: At the time she offers suggestions.

- Where: Where will her advice be used? At school.

- Why: In order to be more helpful to John.

- How: How is she going to find out how to help him? By asking some questions.

So when you are communicating with your child, you can be that thorough so there is no misunderstanding between the two of you. Just imagine how much better your communication would be just by keeping these six questions in mind. You may be thinking this will be hard to remember. Well, anything is hard to remember at first. The first time you rode a bike, you fell off a few times. But once you got used to it, it was second nature. This is something you get used to doing, and then all of a sudden it is automatic. Just like when I was going to the pool with my family. When I started getting anxious, that was my trigger to go through and answer the six questions to bring my anxiety down, simply by reducing the number of unknowns.

Plan B

Here are the six questions to ask John to help him identify and refine his beliefs about the advice that he has been given. I'm going to leave out John's answers because the questions here are the focus of the strategy.

Mary will ask John this series of questions:

- What advice have you been hearing me give to you, John? I ask this because I don't think I did enough to make sure I explained it as well as you needed me to.

- When I give you these suggestions, do you feel that following them will help you in any way?

- What problems (if any) do you think would be caused if you follow these suggestions?

- What (if anything) have you experienced that makes you think those things will happen?

- What would you like to have happen if you follow my suggestions and they worked, John?

- What do you do if it does not go as planned?

The last question is very important because, as I mentioned before, social strategies are usually taught as if they are going to work and a lot of spectrumites are really thinking: What if it doesn't, what if I look bad, what if they bully me? By asking the last question in the list above you address that concern and can then help your child create a Plan B. If Plan A goes wonderfully, great, you have social success. But what if it doesn't go that well? How do you exit gracefully without looking bad? Every child needs a Plan B, but is seldom taught one. It is amazing how quickly things have shifted in the lives of my clients when I introduced the process of a Plan B to them.

Let me give you an example: I consulted with a father and son who love to go fishing together. There was an occasion when the father said they would go fishing the next day. Guess what happened the next day? It rained all day, but in the son's mind, fishing was going to happen. His father said they couldn't because it was raining. The son became very angry at the father, called him a liar, and said he couldn't trust him because he didn't keep his promise. The only thing that mattered to him was the agreement he made with his father. So I introduced his father to the following approach: "If you plan on fishing one day, also plan on an alternative in the event that fishing can't happen."

One thing I want to make sure you understand is the reality that there are a variety of contingencies that could prevent fishing; it could be raining, there could be a flat tire and there is no spare, one of them might get sick and need to stay home. There could be a lot of reasons why it couldn't happen, and guess what, you can't account for all the reasons it might not happen, so there is no point explaining your plan B in a specific way, such as, "If it isn't raining, we'll go fishing." All you need to know is that in the event it does not happen, for whatever reason, you plan to do something specific instead. So the father took my suggestion and the next time they planned to go fishing, they had a Plan B to work on model airplanes together. When the time came to implement that Plan B, there was no meltdown, arguing, or fighting because the two agreements were made and agreed to: We are either going fishing or building model airplanes, and because one of them was delivered on, no lies were told, and no promises were broken. That is why the "What do you do if it doesn't go as planned?" is so essential. It provides a solution to a significant social unknown, it can help reduce anxiety, prevent a meltdown and it also maintains trust between the parent and the child.

The importance of why

A statement I hear frequently from parents is: "I just want my son to be obedient. I wish he would stop asking why all of the time. I wish he would just do what is asked." My question to those parents is, what is the value of blind obedience? Why aren't they allowed to ask why? There's an incredibly valuable purpose in asking why. Let me explain from the spectrumite's standpoint. The most critical set of skills and strategies any person needs are the ones required for problem solving, and we know how difficult it is for our kids to solve problems. So every time a child or an adult on the spectrum, an employee or a spouse on the spectrum, or anybody else asks you why, it gives you a chance to explain what problem will be solved by them doing what is asked.

If she has difficulty solving problems, this is her golden opportunity to learn that she can do it. Explain the problem that will be solved for you by her assistance. If there is anything a spectrumite needs to build up her confidence, it is the repeated experience of solving problems competently.

One mother explained that her son gets angry when asked to do something and asks the same question each time, "Why do I have to do this?" She stated that he responds this way to the same requests, so it isn't that he doesn't know why he's being asked, he simply doesn't want to. The specific example she offered was the extra schoolwork she has him do over the summer so he doesn't regress. She wants to make sure he has an easier transition when the new school year starts. So every day during the summer she works with him on math and English. Every day he asks why he has to do math because he doesn't like math. I asked her to tell me how she answers the question, "Why do I have to do math, I don't like math?"

She tells him that we use math every day, everyone uses math in some capacity every day. Eventually they are able to get through the math problems, but each day he asks the same question. Here, in my opinion is what's missing: She's giving him an answer but she's not answering his question. He is asking, "Why do *I* have to do this?" When she says, "Well, everybody uses math every day," she's talking about everybody but him. Why does it solve a problem for him, and why does he need to know this? How would his life be any worse if he didn't know this stuff?

I suggested that she make math more applicable and have some part of his everyday life require him to use what it is he is being taught. For example, my nine-year-old struggles with schoolwork. He happens to love helping Mom bake. You need to use measuring spoons when baking. So if he wants to help bake, he also needs to understand the process and the tools involved in baking. You could even experiment and show him how things turn out with math and without it.

It is important to make the value of learning personal, especially for a very subjective spectrumite. You've got to find a way to make it relevant to his experience. If it causes him a problem to not know it, then he'll be more invested in it. But if you keep talking about it in future terms of needing it someday, for a child who lives in the present, the idea of someday does not compute. Find a way to bring it into his everyday experience and show him that not knowing it causes him a problem.

What's the solution?

This next strategy is the one I use to break myself, my clients, and my children out of the pessimistic cycles we tend to get ourselves into. I remember being told throughout my childhood that I was my own worst enemy. One of my teachers gave me a book called *The Power of Positive Thinking*. I didn't see any use in that at all and it was probably just a book of fairytales in my mind. I was that negative, even into my adulthood. I remember working myself into panic attacks and sometimes into periods of depression because I saw everything so negatively.

Then I reached a point where I became so sick of being out of control, feeling helpless all of the time, that it finally occurred to me that the way to stop being so overwhelmed by all of these problems was to learn how to solve them. Now, whenever I find myself starting to think in a problem-focused way, I ask myself a very simple question that shifts my thinking from reacting to something to deciding on what action to take, and from thinking about everything that isn't working to what will work. Any guesses what the question is?

The question I ask myself is: What's the solution? I ask myself this question over and over again until the negative thinking slows down and stops. Identifying a problem and then contemplating all of the additional problems that will occur if the original problem happens or remains unsolved is what drives negative thinking. But when you keep asking, "What's the solution?" you take all the energy away from the problem and commit it to the solution.

A parent asked, "What if the negativity is such that the reaction is that there is no solution and the spiral has already reached bottom?" Believe it or not, when somebody tells me there is no solution, I continue to ask, "What's the solution?" I have had clients who think in full catastrophe mode. Sometimes I mix it up a little bit and ask, "How do you benefit from continuing to think like this?", "What do you gain from this by continuing to think the sky is falling?", "What problem does it solve for you to be so frightened all of the time?" It is possible that thinking things won't work out solves the problem of whether to take the risk of trying something new. So that is in fact a solution. Exploring their thinking in this way still gives you something you can work with in terms of thinking of solutions. A little reverse psychology if you will.

Sometimes a person will wear himself out with the negativity, and when he does, I ask him if he is ready to discuss other options for looking at the situation. In some cases, "What's the solution?" involves realizing he doesn't know the solution but maybe somebody else does.

Then a discussion of self-advocacy begins to help him determine how he'd let his needs for a solution be known. Some form of, "There's a problem, and I need a solution for it. I don't know what it is, and I think that you may, but if you don't, do you know somebody who does because I'd really like a solution?" Asking, "What is the solution?" has become such a powerful tool for me that it is the first thing I ask myself whenever there is a problem now. It has been particularly useful in raising my children.

I have three spectrum boys, as you know, and each one of them at any given point can get stuck in a negative cycle, worrying about something, becoming catastrophic, "Everything is awful, the world hates me, why don't I just die." They get stuck in that thinking every now and then, and I need to be able to lead them out of it. Being raised on the steady diet of criticism, as spectrumites often are, they tend to think of themselves as people who cause problems, not people who solve them. How can you blame them, with feedback like, "Look at what you did, you messed up again, why don't you ever listen to me, why do you keep doing it that way when I told you a hundred times do it a different way?"

Even when you offer them solutions, your premise is that they somehow caused the problem. Which requires someone to have to solve it. These kids are used to thinking that they are problem causers, not problem solvers. It is critical that you begin to shift your own thinking to focus on the solution; that is what the both of you really want after all. They typically get angry because there is a problem they don't know how to solve but the moment you start asking, "What's the solution?" you open up that dialogue.

This is why so many spectrumites avoid problems instead of solving them. I work with many clients in their teens and twenties that avoid, avoid, avoid. Their parents advise them that if they procrastinate, it will just get worse, but they continue to avoid it. That's because for their entire lives they have been repeatedly reminded that they don't know how to solve problems, so they just avoid them. Well, we all know that problems don't go away; they get bigger and they accumulate. The one way to begin shifting that thinking from problem avoidance to being proactive is for them to be given opportunities to participate in solving problems.

It amazes me how often, when I ask parents what they do when their children won't do what's asked after several requests, they say, "Well, I end up doing it." What they're telling me is that they're upset that their child won't help out or take responsibility while simultaneously sending the message that if he simply waits long enough, they'll do it for him. I'd say they're teaching him some wonderful problem solving. He's learning that the solution to a problem he wants to avoid is found by avoiding it long enough that his parents become impatient and do it for him. Does this sound familiar?

Reaping what you sow

On an ordinary Sunday morning my two eldest sons, then ages eleven and seven, came into our bedroom and announced they would be making breakfast for the whole family. The seven-year-old meticulously set the table—knives, forks, he even went as far as to wrap the utensils in napkins just like he saw it done at the restaurant. My eleven-year-old cooked the bacon and didn't burn it, and then he and the seven-year-old combined their efforts to crack and scramble the eggs. How do you think this all happened? Why do you think they were compelled to do this? Were they inspired by repeatedly being told how they were always messing up and being allowed to avoid problems until someone else solved them?

Let me explain what led to this event. My eldest son Zach, now thirteen, loves bacon. My now nine-year-old son Aidan loves scrambled eggs. If they want to eat their favorite food, doesn't it make sense that they should know how to make it? When Aidan would ask to have eggs, I'd say, "I suppose so, but how are scrambled eggs made?" The problem is that he wants scrambled eggs. The solution begins with asking, "How do they get made?" When his response is, "I don't know," I reply, "Let's find out." So we go into the kitchen and go step by step, beginning with what we need and then what to do with it when we have it all together. From the preparation to the cooking, the eating, and the cleaning up, if he wants scrambled eggs, he needs to be involved in the whole process. With each step, there is a new problem to be solved, so I continually ask him what's next until the process is complete.

Utilizing the six questions—Who, What, When, Where, Why, and How—works beautifully in facilitating this kind of learning as well. For example: Who wants the eggs? You want the eggs. Where are the eggs? What do we need to make the eggs? Why are we making eggs? How do we make them?

We use the six questions to define the problems and "What's the solution?" to keep moving until they're solved. Isn't it nice how all of these strategies overlap and work synergistically together? This process is all about giving him those opportunities to solve problems instead of simply doing it for him. So many adults want to be helpful and take care of our kids, but it is often at the expense of their own competence. There are problems they can be actively involved in solving that we don't give them the opportunity to help solve. Instead we inadvertently encourage them to remain helpless when they can actually be helpful.

At ages eleven and seven, after extensive experience in the process of making breakfast from start to finish, Zach and Aidan decided to make breakfast and they did a wonderful job. We were shocked because it was the first time they had taken it all on by themselves. We had always been involved somehow, but they realized they had answers to all six questions, they knew all the steps and wanted to do it so they did.

Aidan has embraced his competence in the kitchen to such an extent that around his eighth birthday we bought him a chef's hat. For quite some time he wouldn't cook anything in the kitchen unless he was wearing it. Whereas he struggles in school and historically has received a lot of criticism for not trying harder, he knows that when he is in the kitchen, he is competent. He loves being in a room where he feels he can solve problems, and it is wonderful to see him glowing with pride because of it.

After sharing this story with one mother she asked, "Why do spectrumites avoid finding solutions when it will make things so much better?" I explained that when people are so used to things not working and have so few experiences of it ever working, it occurs to them that working to solve problems is a waste of time and that they will probably end up with the problem remaining and a feeling of being defeated and incompetent once again.

I helped my sons overcome that by partnering with them in a way that showed the process we were going through together was going to work. Because they played a role in it, they shared responsibility for the success. Enough of those experiences and suddenly problem solving becomes a doable and exciting proposition.

Asking, "What's the solution?" over and over again helps identify and learn the process. That is why it is important for you to facilitate experiences of competence with your child. When she doesn't know what solutions exist and you do, you can get her to hang in there by saying, "Oh, that didn't work. I see you're frustrated. But guess what? There's a solution and I know we are going to find it. We are in this together." You are her partner along that journey, and she is not on her own. If you support her through the process, you are going to say, "See, we got there. Yes, it took a little while and maybe it was frustrating at some points, but we stuck with it and found the solution." This process is very effective.

As her parent or teacher you are her model for how problems get solved. You are also her partner in solving that problem instead of her rescuer. Teach her how to solve problems with somebody else instead of thinking she needs to do it all the time on her own, or that somebody needs to do it for her.

Too often, a win–lose mind-set leads to two options for problem solving: either they do it alone or you do it for them, but you don't do it together. The purpose of relationships is connection and partnership, and that's what these strategies are for: creating that partnership and negotiating how you work together effectively instead of in competition with each other. Through partnership, you learn to collaborate on finding solutions you both care about.

Let's review

Before I discuss the final strategy, I want to review the other strategies we've discussed to this point. As we review them, think about how well they overlap and complement each other. Remember, these are some of the best tools for creating the win–win relationship with your child that you both need.

1. *How am I doing?* This is the feedback question we all have running through our heads that lets us know whether we are effective in our environment, relationships, and life.

2. *Clarification.* This is the number one way to measure whether what was meant is what was actually heard and understood. You don't know you were understood when someone says, "I understand." You can't tell by his or her body language because that is unreliable. The only way you are going to actually know what a person meant is by clarifying the action he'll take based on his understanding.

3. *Negotiation.* That's the way two people agree to the rules of how to do their relationship. Negotiation is an agreement of how to do "We" and the partnership.

4. *You, Me, and We.* This is the understanding that relationships can only work if they meet the needs of you and me, and especially improve the partnership between the two of you. It is not good enough if it works for only one person, because if it doesn't improve the relationship, it's ignoring the We.

5. *Three G's.* This is the simple formula of Goal, Give, and Get. When you begin every conversation, have a specific outcome in mind—you need a plan for *giving* the information the other person needs in order to understand

your *goal*, and you need to determine the questions you are going to ask to *get* the information you need. That is my reciprocity formula. I use it all the time and it works very well.

6. *Self-advocacy.* How do you ask for help and get it? If it was as simple as raising your hand, everybody would do it, and that's where I describe the five steps required to effectively ask for and get the help you need, the way you need it, and when you need it.

7. *Touch and Go.* This strategy allows spectrumites to engage sensorially overwhelming environments by devising a plan for engaging and disengaging so that they can last longer in those situations without melting down. It would be nice if all our children were allowed this in school instead of, "You must be in class and stay in class." They often aren't allowed Touch and Go; but are forced to do *touch* at their own expense and get overloaded. We shouldn't have to wait until adulthood to discover and benefit from this strategy. We need to learn it earlier as spectrumites in order to be respectful to ourselves and learn how to regulate our own energy and the intensity of life. Our childhood memories should not be a list of meltdowns; they should include positive experiences and lessons in how to respect ourselves, take care of ourselves and experience our own competence.

8. *Social disclaimers.* This is one of my favorites because it allows me to explain to others why I avoid things like eye contact when talking to them and they never give it a second thought. This also helps to make conversations less painful and more enjoyable. A quick example for the social disclaimer is: "Oh, by the way it really helps me hear you a lot better if I turn my ear towards you, so if I'm doing that, you know why." That eliminates the awkward curiosity as to why you are not looking them in the eye. Doesn't that

make more sense than forcing myself to look someone in the eye when it does nothing but cause me pain and interfere with effective listening? So social disclaimers are very helpful in that respect.

9. *Six questions for a 360 degree conversation: Who, What, When, Where, Why, and How.* These questions are used to understand the facts and needs of a situation as thoroughly as possible.

10. *What's the solution?* The powerful question that breaks the cycle of negativity so you can begin to work at solving problems instead of fixating on them.

Where to go from "no"

Last but not least, "Where to go from 'no'" is the final strategy in this book. "No" is one of those words that you think is clear, easy to understand, and not requiring further explanation, and yet, what is the reaction you get when a spectrumite hears *no*? In some cases they throw a tantrum, may argue more, and even fly into a rage. In my experience many spectrumites seem devastated as if they never saw it coming. Feeling abandoned or rejected by you is a common experience. So, why is there such a strong reaction?

Let's begin with our beliefs; if you don't believe it, you won't do it. Let's talk about what the word "no" means to some people. For some, the word "no" doesn't mean "no." They hear it as something more open-ended as in, "Oh, well, I guess she means not now, or maybe later, or come back and check with me in a few minutes." Some spectrumites I work with seem to respond with, "You must not have heard me right and I must continue to badger you until you understand your station in life is to give me what I want." Do you know anyone like this?

The reality for us is that it is neither possible nor reasonable to give a person everything he or she wants all of the time. We just don't have the resources. Since it is so easy for some to hear the word "no" however they choose—it could mean "not now, but maybe later"—it is imperative to understand what the spectrumite in your life believes about that word before using it. What does your child believe the word "no" means? I worked with a child who could seriously guilt-trip his mother when she wouldn't buy him everything he asked for. He'd say, "You don't love me because if you did you'd want me to be happy." We'll discuss a strategy for countering comments like that.

For now, consider whether you've taken the time to examine whether you and your child define "no" the same way. When someone on the spectrum asks something of you and you know you are going to say "no," this is one way to prevent the rage and the meltdown from even beginning. You are going to be surprised how simple this is.

What if I said "no"?

When a child approaches you and asks you for something, you ask this: "Let me ask you something. If I were to answer your question by saying 'no,' what would that mean to you?" If you were to ask that of your child, what kinds of answers do you think you would get? Do you think he would be sad? Let me tell you what kind of answers I have received from my own sons.

I have heard things like, "Well, it would mean that you hate me," "You don't want me to be happy," "You don't love me and that I'm a bad kid," "It would make me sad," or, "It would be unfair if you said *no*." None of the answers they give are in an angry tone because I didn't say *no* yet; I just asked the question "What if I said *no*?" At most they sound a little impatient or frustrated.

My children have now told me what that word means to them. Try getting it out of them after you have already said "no" and they're melting down or in a rage. They might say, "You're mean, I hate you." Doesn't it make sense to know the belief first, because if you know how your child is going to hear it, then you know how to frame your answer?

The "yes" solution

Why might a spectrumite be devastated by the word *no* as though he never expected to hear it? For someone who needs everything to work because typically his life is filled with problems instead of solutions, what is a "yes" answer? A "yes" is a solution. He comes to you with a need and a "yes" will satisfy that need and solve that problem without having to do any problem solving. It is simple so he comes to you thinking that "yes" is the only possible option, because in a world filled with problems a "yes" answer will solve all of them. That is why a "yes" is so important to him.

This of course is the result of years of having people solve problems for you. If you say "no" to a child who is used to others solving her problems, she may feel abandoned. I know that sounds extreme, but for a child who feels helpless without you, it can seem that way sometimes. She has come to you to solve a problem and she doesn't know how to do it but you do—but you told her "no" again, so now whom can she count on? She thinks, "If I can't count on you to solve my problems, nobody can help me." This is a situation where "What's the solution?" can be used. Just recently I used this with my eldest son, Zach. He wanted me to buy yet another video game for him. I told him, "I know you want it, but the money you want me to spend on it needs to be spent on other things such as groceries. So if you don't want to eat, then we can get your game." Though he's a picky eater, he still wants to eat, but he also wants the game.

My question to him was, "If you want both and I need to spend my money on food, what's the solution?" or, "How do we get the money?" He said, "I can do some extra chores around the house." I clarified that I'd still have to pay him with grocery money, so I encouraged him to think of additional solutions. He called his grandmother to ask her for ideas. As it turns out, my parents were planning on leaving for a multiweek vacation and asked him if he'd like to earn money by mowing their lawn while they were gone. He agreed and had his solution.

So I didn't tell him "no," I just told him I wasn't going to create the solution for him, but I did support him in finding a solution. Remember that these strategies take time to make a routine part of how you and your child communicate. The first few times it's important to expect some pushback because a new approach means you're changing the routine. You're renegotiating the relationship. You might ask, "How are you going to earn this?" Then the response you get is that he ignores you and walks away. A short time later he returns and asks, "OK, when are you going to get it for me?" It isn't that he didn't hear you the first time, he is simply following the old script the two of you had and he only knows his lines for that conversation. He needs some explanation on the new conversation you're having.

When he continues to ask, "So when are you going to take me to buy this?" You can respond, "As soon as we determine how you're going to afford it." You are explaining that you want to explore an option other than solving the problem for him. In a win–win relationship both people have to get something. If you're going to do your part and drive him there, he needs to determine how he will pay for it.

He'll be frustrated at first because this is a new process, and once you start doing this more routinely, it should get easier and he should have more success with it. And point out to him that the sooner he gets on board with the win–win solution, the sooner he gets what he wants. If he continues to resist, you can encourage him to reflect on how sticking with the old way is sabotaging his ability to get what he wants. Ask him, "Is it causing you a problem to not answer the question? Because the more you do not answer the question, the longer you go without this toy. Is that correct?" So if he wants to solve the problem about having the toy, he can answer the question of how he is going to earn it. Think of it in terms of problems and solutions; he thinks currently that giving in to you is causing him a problem when he doesn't realize that actually going along with the win–win option will solve the problem.

Accepting "no"

Let's examine the "no" answer more deeply. So far we've discussed, "How would you take it if I said 'no'?" and a child has said, "I would get mad or angry." Well, now you understand the belief but you haven't changed his belief yet. Because if he says he will get mad and start throwing stuff, now you know what's coming so when you do say "no," you get exactly what's predicted. You need to shift his understanding of "no" so that doesn't happen.

It is important to realize that the process of helping him hear the word "no" without melting down requires the use of the ten main strategies we've already discussed. Let me walk you through how such a dialogue might look between Mary and John. It begins with clarifying whether John has considered an answer other than "yes" before making his request.

John makes a request and Mary asks, "Is there a particular answer you are expecting to get to this question, or can I answer the way I want to?"

JOHN: You're supposed to say "yes."

MARY: If I'm unable to give you what you want and I have to say "no," what then?

JOHN: I will be very mad and I'll break things.

MARY: Oh, so you'll get mad and break things, is that correct?

Mary is using a combination of clarification and the Three Gs. She is using statements and questions to clarify her goal, which is to determine how John will respond to the answer "no."

JOHN: Yes.

MARY: Do you think getting mad and breaking things will make me want to give you what you want?

JOHN: No.

Now Mary begins moving into the negotiation.

MARY: So if getting mad and breaking things won't make me want to give you what you want, then what will?

JOHN: Being nice.

MARY: You're right. I like when you are nice to me. So if my answer to your question is "no," how can you be nice to me?

JOHN: By not getting mad.

MARY: Actually, I can understand if you get a little upset. You know, I get upset when I don't get what I want, but how do you be nice to me when you are upset?

JOHN: Well, I'd say I'm mad but not break things.

MARY: Is that something you think you can do?

JOHN. I think so.

MARY: Would you like to practice?

JOHN: OK.

MARY: Now, ask me your question again and I am going to say "no" and then you respond the way you just said you would.

Let's proceed as though John and Mary's practice went smoothly. Now Mary clarifies with John to help him understand the results he got from the new approach. It helps him answer the question "How am I doing?" differently when he hears the word "no."

MARY: That was great! Did you get what you wanted?

JOHN: No.

MARY: Is there anything else you didn't get?

JOHN: I didn't get in trouble.

MARY: Why not?

JOHN: Because I was nice.

MARY: So, you didn't get what you asked for but you also didn't get in trouble?

JOHN: Right.

Now Mary will apply the You, Me, and We strategy.

MARY: Are you happier when we talk to each other this way?

JOHN: Yes.

MARY: I'm happier, too, because when we talk to each other this way, you get to be treated nicely instead of punished, I get to feel like you respect me more, and we can feel good about talking to each other instead of fighting. Does this sound more fair to you?

JOHN: Yes, it does.

Mary then uses elements of self-advocacy with the Three Gs.

MARY: So from now on, our goal is to be nice to each other even if I say "no" when you ask me for something. Will that work for you?

JOHN: Yes.

MARY: Now let's say you ask me to buy you something you really, really want and you are expecting to get a "yes" but you get a "no," then what do you give me when you get a "no" from me?

JOHN: I will say OK.

MARY: Then how do we get to feel about talking to each other?

JOHN: We get to feel happy. But what if I really want it?

MARY: Then we can talk about it and you can explain to me why you feel it would help you to get what you want, and we will figure out if there is some way you can get it. How does that sound?

JOHN: Great!

So that would allow Mary to use "What's the solution?" when helping John figure out another way to get what he wants. Now Mary will discuss Touch and Go with John as a Plan B in case one of them forgets the agreement they just made about how to talk to each other.

MARY: Now, here is something to think about, John. What if one of us forgets our agreement and we get mad and end up being mean to each other?

JOHN: I don't know. Do we get in trouble?

MARY: We might unless we figure out a way to remember our deal.

JOHN: How do we do that?

MARY: We agree that if one of us gets mad, the other person can ask to take a five-minute break. That way the person who got mad can calm down. Then we can start again but this time by keeping our deal.

JOHN: I like that.

Now, of course, this conversation between John and Mary can go on and on, but I hope I've given you enough to understand the process. Once you are more familiar with these strategies, and internalize the beliefs behind them, what you are working to accomplish, what experience you are working to have, then you'll be better able to build the partnership between you and your child that you need.

Let me clarify the spirit of the dialogue I've just described between Mary and John. As parents, we don't enjoy being spoken to hurtfully by our children. When your child gets angry with you and gets punished, that's a win–lose approach in which the opportunity to negotiate a way that will work for both of you gets lost. His anger is just a child's way of letting you know how unfairly treated he feels, and he wants to punish you and doesn't realize that what he is doing is sabotaging himself.

So your objective is to let him know that you want to help him get what he wants and want him to feel supported and happy, but the way he is showing you his anger is not going to get it for him. Feeling angry is perfectly human, but showing it to you in that way, by telling you he is going to kill you or break things, doesn't make you want to support him. Then you negotiate how he can be angry but tell you in a way that you can still support him so it is a win–win. That is what the negotiation is for.

This conversation takes place over time, especially for a child with a short attention span. The conversation between Mary and John had a strong foundation that you will need to build as well. At first your child may just keep walking away. Let her. She may need a little Touch and Go. She'll be back. When she comes back you can ask if there is something you can help her with? If she reinitiates the conversation, then you can continue it. Begin by clarifying why she walked away by asking, "Did you just need a break or didn't you like the answer you got?"

Then if she walks away again or refuses to discuss it with you, you clarify more: "OK, so I am understanding correctly, are you saying you want no part of this solution and you want the decision to be made without you, or are you just taking a break and you want to come back when you are ready?"

This has worked for me because I make it clear that leaving repeatedly could result in losing entirely by refusing to engage. Usually what my kids say to me is, "No, I just need a break," or, "Fine, I'll stay." But you need to verbalize the options they're exercising because they aren't considering them. You are providing them with Plan A and Plan B. Plan A is "If you are leaving, you can lose everything." Plan B is "Take a break, come back, and be part of the solution."

We certainly have discussed a lot in this book and even with all this there is still so much more to learn. We are all in this together and as I learn more I will gladly share it with you. May you partnerships be strong and fulfilling, you deserve it. Keep moving forward.

Glossary

ADD/attention deficit disorder: A condition making focused attention difficult to maintain to such an extent that learning, memory, and socialization are noticeably impacted.

Aspie: A term used by those with Asperger's syndrome as a less pejorative description of their eccentric way of being.

Bang and crash: Rough play in which one enjoys the feeling of impact.

Dysgraphia: Poor fine motor coordination that effects handwriting and the use of precision objects such as eating utensils. The physical act of writing can be very tiring and frustrating.

Dyspraxia: Difficulty moving the body in a coordinated way, resulting in clumsiness in walking and running, frequently bumping into things, and knocking things over. It can be accompanied by low muscle tone.

Executive functioning: Cognitive abilities involved in organizing, prioritizing, and problem solving.

Expressive language: Written and verbal communication.

Hyperfocus: Concentrating so completely on an object or activity that one is unable to be distracted or perceive sensory stimuli in the environment.

Hypersensitivity: An overwhelming sensation resulting from specific sensory input, resulting in anxiety around anticipated exposure to that input.

Hyposensitivity: A sensory experience one seeks in intensity or duration in order to feel that that experience has occurred.

IEP/Individualized Education Plan: A federally mandated legal document that provides accommodations to a student whose disability would negatively impact his or her education without such accommodations in place.

Neurotypical: The average person with no known label denoting a disability.

OCD/obsessive-compulsive disorder: An anxiety disorder characterized by obsessive thoughts that result in excessive worry. This worry is relieved or managed by compulsive repetitive behaviors or routines.

Parallel play: Play that is side by side, not interactive.

Proprioception: The sense of where one's own body and limbs are in space.

Receptive language: Comprehension of language.

Spectrumite: A term used to refer to individuals on the autism spectrum.

Stimming: A repetitive body movement or sound used to help regulate one's own nervous system.

Supersensitivity: A sensory experience that creates an overwhelming experience of pain the moment it is experienced.

Synesthesia: A neurological condition in which the experience of one sensory pathway triggers a sensory experience in another. For example, hearing music simultaneously results in seeing color associated with each musical note. Another example would be experiencing a specific smell in response to hearing certain sounds.

Unitasking: Committing to completing one task at a time.

Vestibular: The sensory system that determines the direction of movement such as linear or rotation.

References

King, B. (2004) *What to Do When You're Totally Screwed: Simple Strategies for Bringing Your Life into Balance.* Lincoln, NE: iUniverse, Inc.

Shore, S. (2003) *Beyond the Wall: Personal Experiences with Autism and Asperger's Syndrome.* Shawnee Mission, KS: Autism Asperger's Publishing Company.

Willey, L.H. (1999) *Pretending to Be Normal: Living with Asperger's Syndrome.* London: Jessica Kingsley Publishers.